The Doughboys of San Joaquin County

Published by Tuleburg Press

Stockton, CA

www.tuleburgpress.com

tuleburpress@gmail.com

ISBN 978-1-7321347-4-4

Cover Photograph:

Corporal Aubrey E. Dixon , 254th Aero Service Squadron

Shotwick Airfield, Cheshire, England

(photo courtesy of the author)

This project was funded in part by the CB Merchant Services Charitable Fund

THE DOUGHBOYS OF SAN JOAQUIN COUNTY

*Their lives, their stories and
their names on a wall...*

**Written by
Elaine Dixon-Ugarkovich**

TABLE OF CONTENTS

FOREWORD

I have always loved history; and as an amateur genealogist, I love entwining people's stories into context with our history. My grandfather served in World War 1, and later I would inherit his uniform and collection of photos and postcards. He used to tell us about being an airplane mechanic during the war. The story seemed so odd. "Grandpa, did they really have airplanes way back then?" "Yes Elaine, they did," he would reply. It was his story.

One evening while attending a function at the Stockton Memorial Civic Auditorium, my husband pointed out a plaque. On it were the names of the young men from San Joaquin County who had died in the First World War. I took a picture with my phone; and later that night, I carefully examined it. I was intrigued. Who were these young men? What were they doing in 1917 when our country entered the fray? Who were their families? And how did they die?

I later learned there was a second plaque with names of men from the City of Stockton. I now had 122 names. But to me, they weren't just names. They were stories, and someone needed to tell them. I felt a tug at my heart and knew that I was going to be the one to write their stories.

So I put on my genealogist hat and began scouring records. I read census records, city directories, draft registration cards, military transport manifests and, most importantly, obituaries. I kept a notebook filled with data. I learned about men whose families had been in the area since the Gold Rush. I found new immigrants who spoke little English. I found college graduates and some with only a few years of schooling. I discovered farmers, clerks and railway workers. But most of all, I discovered families who mourned the loss of a son – and communities who mourned with them.

These are their stories…

This book is dedicated to my grandfather

Corporal Aubrey Ernest Dixon

254th Aero Service Squadron

American Expeditionary Forces

born in Sacramento, raised in Elk Grove,
farmed in Thornton, died in Lodi

(1887-1966)

Thank you for your service

THE DOUGHBOYS OF SAN JOAQUIN COUNTY

With a jubilant send-off from a city of proud citizens, 39 young men boarded the train for Camp Lewis, Washington. With shouts of "On to Berlin" and "Berlin or Bust" and banners of "The San Joaquin's Respects to the Kaiser" and "Watch Us Get Willie," the train chugged down the track. The crowd could be heard yelling "Godspeed" while the Holt Caterpillar band struck up a rendition of "L'Marseillaise." Horns honked, and the crowd cheered amidst falling tears as the train slowly disappeared from their view.

Just minutes earlier, buoyed by patriotic music and civic speeches at Hunter Square, the doughboys had marched down Main Street, turned on El Dorado, swung onto Weber, then south on California to the Southern Pacific Rail Station. It was September 9, 1917. The future soldiers of the newly created National Army were accompanied by members of the Luneta Post of the Veterans of Foreign War, the Home Guard of Stockton, the Eagle Drum Corps, the Stockton High Cadets, the Moose Lodge Drum Corps, the United Spanish War Veterans and veterans of the Grand Army of the Republic. They carried a flag donated by the Rotary Club and were spurred on by the singing of the National Anthem.

Mayor A. C. Oullahan of Stockton proudly stated *"...You, my dear young men, have been called to do a soldier's duty, to defend the flag of your country, the flag of your fathers. Our great country, which we all love more dearly than we love our lives, is in peril and your strong hearts and strong arms will help defend it and keep Old Glory triumphant before all the world...Go where duty calls you, and when you return - God speed the day – we will give you joyful welcome and reward you with evidence of our never-ending gratitude." (The Stockton Record, September 10, 1917)*

SEND-OFF PARADE

BERLIN OR BUST!

(Photos courtesy of Bank of Stockton)

Mayor Oullahan held true to his word. Not only did the city honor those who returned; but more importantly, it honored those who served and gave the ultimate sacrifice.

ONE HUNDRED YEARS HAVE PASSED...

It is important to honor and remember. World War I was called "The Mother's War." The soldiers who completed the first draft registration in June 1917 were between the ages of 21 and 31. To be considered draft eligible, the young man could not be married or be the sole support for his family. He could not be employed in civil service, since the government considered those jobs important to the continued infrastructure of our country. And these young men needed to be fit enough for service.

For the most part, the men did not have children. They did not have anyone to carry on their lineage. Those left to grieve were parents, grandparents, siblings, cousins, nieces and nephews. Because of this unique situation, many of their stories have been lost. They were ordinary men who are today just names on a wall.

THE MEN OF STOCKTON, CALIFORNIA

(Photos taken by Elaine Dixon-Ugarkovich)

THE MEN OF SAN JOAQUIN COUNTY

It is important to remember who they were and why some chose to enlist and fight. They were not ordinary. Here are the stories of their extraordinary lives.

THE WORLD AT WAR

On June 28, 1914, the heir to the Austro-Hungarian throne, Archduke Franz Ferdinand, was assassinated by a Serbian Nationalist. Countries took sides based on current alliances. The Austro-Hungarian government, along with its closest ally, Germany, declared war against the Serbs. Turkey joined them, and the trio became known as the Central Powers. Russia, who needed the shipping lanes of the Black Sea, then declared war on Germany and the Austro-Hungarians. In a domino effect, Great Britain and France supported Russia, and they became known as The Allies. It was now a war for European territory. It was also a "cousins" war since the leaders of England, Russia and Germany were all grandchildren of Queen Victoria.

War waged on for three years, men mired in trenches and fighting with machine guns, snipers and gas. The Allied forces begged for the United States to join them. President Wilson refused. He believed that he was better served as a mediator trying to broker peace. Many Americans disagreed. The United States was becoming wealthy by supplying food, steel, ammunition and money to both sides. Private companies were selling equipment to both sides. Even when the Germans sunk the cruise ship *Lusitania*, with many wealthy Americans aboard, President Wilson held firm to his beliefs.

But in early 1917, things changed. Germany had agreed to keep shipping lanes open since it was on the receiving end of some of our supplies. But angry with American dealings with the Allies, Germany sent what is now known as the *Zimmerman Telegram*. Germany offered financial support to Mexico to invade the southern United States. Mexico at the time was governed by another of Queen Victoria's offspring. The telegram was intercepted by the British, who promptly shared it with President Wilson. At the same time, Germany closed shipping lanes, and U-boats began to torpedo United States merchant ships. President Wilson declared war on Germany and the Central Powers on April 2, 1917. Congress voted in support on April 6, and the United States officially entered the Great War.

The United States did not have a large army. In June, the first wave of only 14,000 soldiers arrived in France. So, lacking a substantial military, the Selective Service was enacted on May 18, 1917. The first registrations were held on June 5, 1917, for those men between the ages of 21 to 31. Overall, ten million men registered.

Attention!

ALL MALES between the ages of 21 and 30 years, both inclusive, must personally appear at the polling place in the Election District in which they reside, on

TUESDAY, JUNE 5th, 1917

between the hours of 7 A.M. and 9 P. M. and

Register

in accordance with the President's Proclamation.

Any male person, between these ages, who fails to register on June 5th, 1917, will be subject to imprisonment in jail or other penal institution for a term of one year.

NO EXCUSE FOR FAILURE TO REGISTER WILL BE ACCEPTED

Each Exemption Board (by county) was given the total number of recruits required from its area. From that June draft, 2.8 million men were selected across the United States, while another two million enlisted. Puerto Rico, which was given US citizenship, and the US Territory of Alaska were both required to draft young men. San Joaquin County's quota was close to 800. Our first contingency, sent on September 9, 1917, was 39 recruits – 5% of the total required.

General John J. Pershing was given command of the American Expeditionary Forces. After months of training in military camps set up around the country, by the summer of 1918, the AEF was landing 10,000 soldiers a day onto French soil.

CAMP LEWIS

American Lake, Pierce County, Washington

THE 91ST DIVISION

Most of the young men from San Joaquin County were assigned to Camp Lewis, which became headquarters to the 91st Division. Constituted on August 5, 1917, Camp Lewis was designated as a major training facility to prepare our men for combat. The goal was to take these farmers, clerks, plumbers and other laborers and turn them into soldiers – soldiers willing to follow orders, no matter what that would entail. Most of the recruits hailed from the Northwestern part of the United States, with the majority from California. Because of their hometown designations, the 91st became known as the Wild West Division. It was under the command of Major General Henry A. Greene.

The National Army was committed to months of training. Despite the United States officially entering the war on April 6, 1917, our Defense Department was not willing to send inexperienced young men to the front. The war had dragged on for three years, so the urgency was not felt by the Americans. War in Europe was being fought in trenches. Battles did not entail much hand-to-hand combat. Our American Expeditionary Forces (AEF), under the command of General John J. "Black Jack" Pershing, had other ideas. In Pershing's January 1918 manual *The Training and Employment of Divisions, 1918,* he wrote, "All training behind the line must be specially directed toward offensive action." But they needed time to ready these men for an offensive action.

The plan was to train the men for six to eight months. During that time men were assigned to Regiments. Some were Infantry, some

Engineers, others would be part of the Signal Corps, while those with shooting skills were assigned to the Machine Gun Battalions. There were Field Artillery, Ammunitions Trains, Sanitary Trains, Supply Trains and Military Police. Finally, there were Medical Regiments, Ambulance and Field Hospitals and those assigned to Headquarters. The 91st was a small city. It became a very large task to prepare all for duty, and marksmanship was of utmost importance.

As training went on and other divisions across the United States were being shipped out, soldiers from the 91st were being transferred to fill spaces. Many were sent to the 41st Division; and by March 2018, the 91st had lost 25% of its men. So, more recruits were sent to Camp Lewis. This replacement scenario caused a huge gap in the level of military skills of each company. Plus, the constant rain in western Washington created health issues resulting in an additional loss of men – some were just sent home, while others died of pneumonia and the common cold.

Now, after almost ten months of training, the 91st began heading overseas to France. Transported to Camp Merritt and shipped out from Hoboken, New Jersey, it arrived in early August. The division was now under the command of Major General William H. Johnston. Troops were sent to camps for additional training and later were assigned to the French Forces acting as reserve. Their first test was at the battle of St. Mihiel on September 12, 1918. Their first interaction with the enemy lasted just three days and ended on September 15. No longer "wet behind the ears," the 91st felt it was ready. But three days does not a war make.

General Pershing made the decision to send the 91st to the front of battle despite its lack of fighting experience. On September 26, 1918, the 361st, 362nd and 363rd Regiments were the first to go "over the top" in the Meuse-Argonne Offensive. The 91st, though not as trained as other divisions, was given the point and advanced farther and faster than the divisions on its flank. After the third day, it had advanced four kilometers ahead of the 37th Division and six kilometers ahead of the 35th Division. It pushed the Germans into retreat, which resulted in high hopes for the Americans.

But the fighting between September 26 and November 11, 1918, would become the largest loss of American life in our military history. Over 26,000 men were killed in action. During the first 46 days of battle, death claimed 24 soldiers who hailed from San Joaquin County. Private Cecil E. Thompson of Escalon was bestowed the Distinguished Service

Cross posthumously for his brave actions while on reconnaissance the night of September 29.

On October 5, the 91st was placed in the rear and given 10 days rest. But Pershing ordered the 182nd Brigade, which included the 363rd and 364th Regiments, to go back into battle, attached to the 1st Division. These men were finally relieved on October 12. Three more men from San Joaquin County were killed in action during that time frame.

On October 15, the 91st was reassigned to the French Forces and sent to Ypres-Lys, Belgium. The division remained there until the end of the war. Again, it was at the center of the fight near Flanders Field. San Joaquin County lost eight more men, including Sergeant Karl E. Ross, who was posthumously awarded the Distinguished Service Cross for his valor.

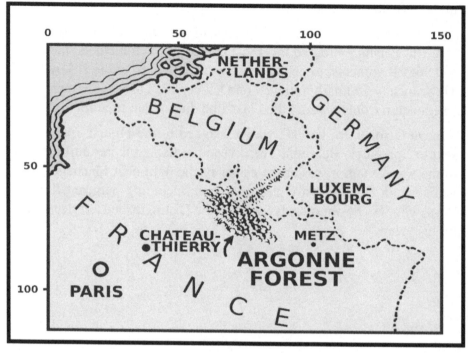

Maps by Pearson Scott Foresman - Wikipedia; Public Domain

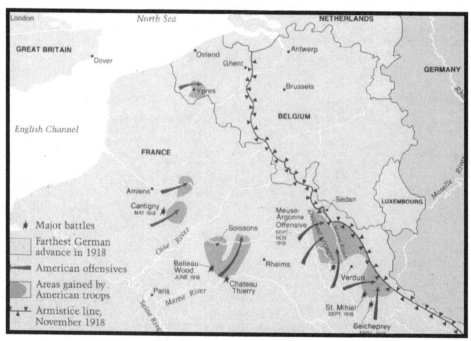

American 100-Day Offensive
Argonne Forest, France and Belgium

THE WILD WEST DIVISION: GREEN FIR TREE ON BROWN BACKGROUND

When the 91st left for the states at the end of the war 4,000 slots had been replaced by men from Ohio. Many were sick and quarantined. It was estimated that 40% of the men remaining in the division were infected with Spanish Influenza.

But the Wild West Division had left its mark on history. It was known as a division that fought with valor and intensity. It was impassioned more than skilled. It captured 33 enemy artillery, 471 machine guns, and 2,412 prisoners. One hundred fifty members were awarded the Belgian Croix de Guerre, including Chester Mason, Peter Sievers and Oliver Wallace from San Joaquin County. Others were given the French Croix de Guerre, and many were the recipient of our country's second highest military honor – the Distinguished Service Cross. Four of those men - Cecil Thompson, Karl Ross, Perry Schurr and Harold Strother - came from San Joaquin County.

Local soldiers who served in the 91st Division and lost their lives:

Sergeants: Ralph Gillespie, Carl R. B. Gustafson, George L. McCall, Clinton McCausland, Hope McFall, Karl E. Ross, William I. Tredway

Corporals: Herbert H. Adams, Jerrold J. Aggeler, Harold E. Cary, Paul R. Holdzkum, Thomas W. Hugill, Edward H. Lorensen, James H. Mead, Harold A. Sexton, Guy W. Staples, Lester L. Weylandt, Earl Woodward

Privates: James B. Anderson, Jack Ayk, Ernest M. Bates, William Brennan, Sidney Brown, Frank W. Elsholz, Charles Fontanella, Savio J. Fugazzi, Cornelius Harrison, Edmund Kasper, James G. McDermott, Douglass L. Messersmith, Olaf E. Nelson, Olien O. Rhodes, Dewey D. Sivley, Frank E. Sperry, Oliver J. Stedman, William E. Stone, Cecil E. Thompson, Henry Thorson

Bugler: Charles R. Curry

Many San Joaquin doughboys died in this Great War. Some were killed in action. Some are listed as still missing in action. Others died from the result of being kept as a prisoner of war, while some died from accidents. Some were wounded and died months later after going through extensive treatments or surgeries. And many of our men died from illness – most resulting from the Spanish Influenza pandemic that spread worldwide.

KILLED IN ACTION

Over 4,300,000 men were mobilized by the United States in World War 1. Of that total, approximately 116,500 were killed in action. With the use of gas warfare, heavy artillery and machine guns, the loss of life was great. Here are those with ties to San Joaquin County who lost their lives in battle.

David Crockett Cottrell*	19 Apr 1918	France
Wesley Alan Stone*	23 Apr 1918	Lorraine, France
Herbert Boyer*	5 May 1918	Cantigney, France
Joseph Drabkin	27 May 1918	Flanders Belgium
James Richard Miller	28 May 1918	France
Clyde Wilford Needham	15 Jul 1918	Marne, France
Percy John Fisher	18 Jul 1918	Chateau Thierry, France
Walter Jasper Halstead	19 Jul 1918	Chateau Thierry, France
Arthur S. Vincelet	20 Jul 1918	Chateau Thierry, France
Charles Wiltse Wisthoff	29 Jul 1918	Chateau Thierry, France
Joseph G. Campodonico	8 Aug 1918	Chateau Thierry, France
Adam Klein	12 Aug 1918	France
Vaughn J. Keifer	19 Aug 1918	Belleau, France
Walter Arthur Bicknell	4 Sep 1918	Ligny, France (CEF)
Louis LaFarque	8 Sep 1918	USS Mt Vernon
Clyde Raymond Stamper	12 Sep 1918	St. Mihiel, France
Frank Patnoe	15 Sep 1918	St. Mihiel, France
Harold A. Sexton	20 Sep 1918	Verdun, France

Darrell Collins Mitchell	24 Sep 1918	Oise-Aisne, France
Harold E. Cary	26 Sep 1918	Meuse-Argonne, France
Edmund T. Kasper	26 Sep 1918	Meuse-Argonne, France
Martin Troy, Jr.	26 Sep 1918	Meuse-Argonne, France
Joseph J. Aggeler	27 Sep 1918	Meuse-Argonne, France
John G. Anderson	27 Sep 1918	Meuse-Argonne, France
Charles Fontanella	27 Sep 1918	Meuse-Argonne, France
Carl R. Bertel Gustafson	27 Sep 1918	Meuse-Argonne, France
Edward Hans Lorensen	27 Sep 1918	Meuse-Argonne, France
James G. McDermott	27 Sep 1918	Meuse-Argonne, France
Henry Arne Thorson	27 Sep 1918	Meuse-Argonne, France
Joe Arata	29 Sep 1918	Meuse-Argonne, France
William E. Stone	29 Sep 1918	Meuse-Argonne, France
Lester Lloyd Weylandt	29 Sep 1918	Meuse-Argonne, France
Ralph Gillespie	30 Sep 1918	Meuse-Argonne, France
James Herbert Mead	30 Sep 1918	Meuse-Argonne, France
Hope McFall	1 Oct 1918	Meuse-Argonne, France
Cecil E. Thompson	1 Oct 1918	Meuse-Argonne, France
Will Irving Tredway	1 Oct 1918	Meuse-Argonne, France
Charles Eric Walther	1 Oct 1918	Meuse-Argonne, France
Earl Woodward	1 Oct 1918	Meuse-Argonne, France
Frank W. Elsholz	2 Oct 1918	Meuse-Argonne, France
Paul Holdzkum	2 Oct 1918	Meuse-Argonne, France
Phillip W. Sherlock	2 Oct 1918	Meuse-Argonne. France
Bernard James "Jay" Irwin	3 Oct 1918	Meuse-Argonne, France
Herbert H. Adams	4 Oct 1918	Meuse-Argonne, France
James Budd Anderson	4 Oct 1918	Meuse-Argonne, France
Frank Eugene Sperry	4 Oct 1918	Meuse-Argonne, France
Guy Walter Staples	4 Oct 1918	Meuse-Argonne, France
Leslie M. Roper	8 Oct 1918	Meuse-Argonne, France

Charles Reuben Curry	9 Oct 1918	Meuse-Argonne (Hill 255), France
Herbert Hovard	14 Oct 1918	Meuse-Argonne, France
Thomas Wilbur Hugill	31 Oct 1918	Ypres-Lys, Belgium
Philip B. Montoya	31 Oct 1918	Meuse-Argonne
Karl Erskine Ross	31 Oct 1918	Ypres-Lys Belgium
Clinton McCausland	2 Nov 1918	Ypres-Lys, Belgium
Savio J. Fugazzi	2 Nov 1918	Ypres-Lys, Belgium
Jack Ayk	4 Nov 1918	Ypres-Lys, Belgium
Dewey D. Sivley	5 Nov 1918	Meuse-Argonne, France
Lars P. Larsen	6 Nov 1918	Ypres-Lys, Belgium
Joseph F. Smith	10 Feb 1919	Siberia, Russia
Walter W. Figgins	unknown	France

*The first casualties were men who were early enlistees or were already serving in the military.

DAVID CROCKETT COTTRELL

PFC – Battery E, 146th Field Artillery, 41st Division

David was born in January 1884 in Mariposa County. The family moved to Stockton when his father, Lineus Jasper (L.J.), got a job working at Stockton State Hospital. David's mother had died in 1896, and soon after David went to live with relatives in Rio Vista.

David was the penultimate soldier, having served his country with three enlistments. At age 20 he traveled to Los Angeles and enlisted in the Army on November 7, 1904. He was assigned to a Field Artillery unit in St. Thomas and eventually was attached to the General Hospital at the Presidio in San Francisco. He was honorably discharged on Nov 7, 1907, having fulfilled his three-year commitment. David reenlisted on December 7, 1907, and was assigned to the 3rd Field Artillery, Company D at Fort McDowell, Angel Island.

His company was transferred to Fort Sam Houston, where he served until December 8, 1910. Upon his discharge, he moved to Stockton to be with his father, who resided at 324 N. California Street. In the 1914 City of Stockton Directory, David stated he was working as an engineer.

But when the United States entered World War I in April 1917, David was compelled to enlist again. He joined the 18th Railway Engineers and was sent to American Lake, Washington, for training. After three months, the unit was deployed to France. David shortly thereafter was transferred to Battery E of the 146th Field Artillery, 41st Division.

Not soon after his transfer, PFC Cottrell was exposed to gas warfare. He was sent to an American Army Hospital, where he died on April 19, 1918. Mr. Cottrell later wired the Army Department requesting that David's body be returned to Stockton. He was sent back on October 18, 1920, on the ship *Pocahontas*. He was buried in Parkview Cemetery in Manteca with members of the Native Sons of the Golden West organizing the funeral.

ALAN WESLEY STONE

Corporal – Supply Company C, 2nd Infantry, 5th Regiment, USMC

Alan was born in Arkansas in September 1896 to Tulah Ann Fritts and John Dudley Stone. By the 1910 Census, his family had moved to Stockton and were living in the O'Neil Township on East Clark Road. Sometime later, the family moved into town as they were listed in the 1917 City of Stockton Directory residing at 736 E. 6th Street.

The United States officially entered the war on April 6, 1917. Alan decided immediately that he wanted to serve his country. He enlisted on April 27, 1917, in the United States Marine Corps and was assigned as a Teamster in the 5th Regiment, Supply Company C.

Unfortunately, Alan's service was not long. He was killed in action on April 23, 1918, in Lorraine, France. His father never knew of Alan's fate, as he died on March 9, 1918, and was buried in the Stockton Rural Cemetery.

Alan's body was eventually buried in the St. Mihiel American Cemetery at Thiaucourt, France. He rests in Plot D, Row 22 - Grave 10. His mother was invited by the United States Government to participate in the Mother's Pilgrimage to visit her son's grave, but she declined. Grief-stricken at the loss of both a husband and a son may have influenced her decision.

HERBERT BOYER

Captain – Machine Gun Company (First),
28th Infantry, 1st Division

Herbert was born at 228 Stanislaus Street in Stockton in 1898 to Lulu and John Boyer. As a young boy, he dreamed of a military career. While a young lad in Stockton, he worked for the Flint-Bigelow Company. But in 1916 at age 18, he enlisted at the Presidio in San Francisco. He was assigned to the Quartermaster's Department.

When the United States entered the World War, Herbert was transferred to the First Brigade, Company A, 1st Machine Gun Company, 28th Infantry. He was promoted to 2nd Lieutenant. He took pride in saying that he was the 17th man in the American Expeditionary Forces to set foot on French soil, having arrived on June 17, 1917.

His company was also in the first American Battery sent to the Western Front under the command of General John "Black Jack" Pershing. While serving under General Pershing Boyer was promoted to 1st Lieutenant, and just a week before his death he was given the rank of Captain.

On April 20, 1918, his Company was sent to the front trenches at Seicheprey, in the St. Mihiel Sector. It was there that he was felled by enemy machine gun fire on May 5. He was buried near where he fell. It was extraordinary that he participated in major campaigns for almost a year before giving the ultimate sacrifice.

His body arrived back in Stockton on March 31, 1921, and he was given a hero's burial at Parkview Cemetery in Manteca. Participating in his funeral was the Karl Ross American Legion, the local VFW and the Women's Relief Corps, Legion Auxiliary.

JOSEPH C. DRABKIN

Private – Company I, 164th Infantry, 41st Division

Joseph was born on September 14, 1891, in Shebeseh, Vitebsk, Russia – part of the Grand Duchy of Lithuania and now incorporated into Belarus. His family immigrated to the United States sometime prior to 1917 when Joseph completed his draft registration card.

At that time, his family lived in Lodi at 18 S. School Street. He stated that he was the financial support for his mother, father and sister. He and his brother owned Drabkin Brothers Junk Dealers, which eventually became the Lodi Junk Company.

Joseph was one of the first lads drafted from Lodi and was assigned as a private to the 41st Division, 164th Infantry, Company "I" (most likely as a replacement). The 41st departed for France on December 15, 1917, on the ship *Leviathan*. Sometime during his time in France, "Able" as he was called, was transferred to the 26th Infantry, Company D. He was promoted to Corporal and became the personal liaison to Lt. Wesley Freml.

Company D took heavy shell and gas barrage on Flanders Field in May 1918. Joseph was killed at Montdidier on May 27, 1918, while standing next to Lt. Freml. Corporal Drabkin was buried at the United States Military Cemetery at Villers Tournelle, Somme, France. Freml later would be captured and spend months as a POW.

By 1918, Joseph's brother had moved to Center Street in Stockton. He requested that Joseph's body be exhumed and sent to Stockton. Joseph's final resting place is in the Congregation Adas Yesharan Jewish section of the Stockton Cemetery in French Camp.

JAMES RICHARD MILLER

Private – Supply Company, 162nd Infantry, 41st Division
Private - Company G, 18th Infantry, 1st Division

James was born on June 8, 1891, in Porterville, California. By the 1900 Census, his father had died and his widowed mother, Della, moved to Poplar in Tulare County with her four children. In the 1910 Census, Della again had moved the family. This time, they lived in Woodbridge, just northwest of Lodi. James was working on a farm.

When James completed his 1917 draft registration, he was living with his wife, Myrtle, in Woodbridge, working on his own farm. Originally, Private Miller was assigned to the Supply Company, 162nd Infantry, 41st Division. But while overseas he and Clyde Stamper requested a transfer, stating they were bored and wanted more action. Both were transferred to Company G of the 18th Infantry in the 1st Division.

Private Miller was killed in action on May 27, 1918, at the battle of Somme. He was buried in the Somme American Cemetery, Bony, France, in Plot C, Row 14 - Grave 2.

CLYDE WILFORD NEEDHAM

Corporal – 2ⁿᵈ Battalion, 117ᵗʰ Engineers, 42ⁿᵈ Division

Clyde was born in Acampo, California, on May 27, 1896. His mother, Alice Fuqua, died on July 2, 1896. His father, Clarence C. Needham, in the 1900 Census was living in Acampo. The Census information stated he was a preacher and was widowed. By the 1910 Census, Clarence had remarried and moved to Turlock. Coincidently, the Postmaster of Acampo, Perrin O. Needham, was Clyde's grandfather. It is uncertain why the Needham family did not play an active role in Clyde's life.

Clyde was raised by his maternal grandparents, Francis Marion and Mary Fuqua. The Fuquas had a farm in Acampo, Liberty Township of San Joaquin County. Frank died in 1907, leaving Mary to raise her grandson.

In the 1916 Lodi City Directory, Clyde was working as a driver and lived at 316 E. Locust Street. When he completed his draft registration in 1917, he was a mechanic for Pate & Kise.

Needham was part of the early contingency to depart for Camp Lewis. Having been part of the California National Guard, Needham had prior military experience. In 1916, his 2ⁿᵈ Battalion had supported General Pershing on the US/Mexico border in search of Pancho Villa.

The 2ⁿᵈ Battalion - 117ᵗʰ Engineer Regiment was now attached to the 42ⁿᵈ Division, and Clyde was promoted to Corporal. The 42ⁿᵈ was comprised of elite National Guard units chosen from 26 states. The 117ᵗʰ Engineers from Lodi were now part of the Rainbow Division, given that moniker by their Chief of Staff Colonel Douglas MacArthur. The 42ⁿᵈ participated in 174 days of combat while serving in France.

On July 15, 1918, while in the trenches at the Second Battle of the Marne northeast of Paris, Corporal Needham was hit by a shell. It exploded and killed him instantly. This was the first day of the Spring Offensive, a decisive Allied victory near the Marne River, a battle that included French and American troops.

Corporal Needham eventually was buried in the Meuse-Argonne American Cemetery in Romagne, France. His final resting place is in Plot E, Row 30 - Grave 17.

In February 1922, Clyde W. Needham Elementary in Lodi School District was dedicated in his honor. The school still exists today.

PERCY JOHN FISCHER

Private First Class – Company C,
Signal Corps 1ˢᵗ Battalion, 2ⁿᵈ Division

Percy was born in Stockton on June 21, 1893, to John A. and Ella (Abbott) Fischer. John was born in Switzerland and had immigrated with his parents when he was 17. By 1900, John was widowed and living with his mother in Stockton, so Percy was raised by his grandmother. In 1912, Percy began working as an electrician's helper for the Electric and Manufacturing Equipment Company in Stockton, whilst his father worked at Aurora Mills. When Percy registered for the draft in 1917, he was an electrician for Gould & Johnson Company and lived at 819 E. Anderson Street.

Percy enlisted in the Army in July 1917. He was assigned to Company C of the 1ˢᵗ Battalion's Signal Corps. He was first sent to Fort McDonald and then to Fort Leavenworth, Kansas. Shortly thereafter, the battalion was transported to Camp Vail, New Jersey. The unit departed from New York City on Christmas Eve, 1917, on the White Star Line ship *Lapland*.

Percy was killed in action on July 18, 1918. This was the first day of the Chateau-Thierry and Belleau Woods Campaign. It is unknown how he was killed, but his body was buried near the place where he fell. On May 17, 1921, he was reburied in Parkview Cemetery, Manteca, with full military honors.

WALTER JASPER HALSTEAD

Private – Company C, 59th Infantry, 4th Division

Walter was born in Goshen, California, a small farming town near Visalia, on February 2, 1894. His parents were Jasper Newtown "Dock" Halstead and Georgia Lenz. Walter took a job at Holt Manufacturing Company as a machinist in the jig room and moved to Stockton. He boarded at 845 E. Lindsay Street.

Walter was in one of the early contingents from Stockton who were sent to Camp Lewis. He was assigned to Company G of the 363rd Infantry, 91st Division. Many other young men from San Joaquin County also were assigned to the 363rd. Sometime later, Walter was detached to Company C of the 59th Infantry, most likely as a draft replacement. He was aboard the ship *Megantic* on May 3, 1918, out of New York Harbor with his newly formed company.

The 59th saw early action while under the command of General John "Black Jack" Pershing. One of its first was the battle of Chateau-Thierry in the Aisne-Marne Sector, which began on July 18, 1918. The troops were new and green. Walter was among those killed on July 19, 1918. Unfortunately, the family was not notified of his death until November 28. The family had his body sent to Visalia, and he was buried in the Halstead family plot in Visalia Public Cemetery.

ARTHUR SYLVESTER VINCELET

Private – Company F, 28th Infantry, 1st Division

Arthur was born to Joseph Louis and Caroline (Cook) Vincelet on November 10, 1893 in Davis, California. Soon after his birth, the family moved to Nevada County. His parents divorced sometime before 1906, but they both moved to the Lodi area. His mother lived in the Elkhorn Township, while his father lived in Acampo where he worked as a vineyardist.

In 1917, at the time of the draft, Arthur was living in Acampo (most likely with his father) and worked for Pearly Farms.

Not much is known of Arthur's military career, but he must have been one of the early arrivals in France. He was assigned to the 28th Infantry of the 1st Division and was killed at Chateau Thierry on July 20, 1918. He was buried near where he fell. His body was sent back to Lodi on May 26, 1921, and Private Vincelet was given a final resting place in Lodi Memorial Cemetery. He was interred next to his father, who had died in 1920.

CHARLES WILTSE WISTHOFF

Private – Battery C, 146th Field Artillery, 41st Division

Charles was born to William and Sarah (Wiltse) Wisthoff in Fonda, Iowa, on November 14, 1894. By the 1900 Census, the family had begun to head west, living in Cedar, Iowa. In 1910, they lived on Lower Sacramento Road near Acampo Road in the Liberty Township north of Lodi. William had purchased a farm; and in 1917, Charles stated he was a "farmer on his father's farm."

Charles was William and Sarah's only son. He had two sisters, one who became a nurse at San Joaquin Hospital in French Camp.

On Christmas Eve 1917, Charles found himself on the transport ship *Lapland* (a former White Star Ocean Liner) attached to Battery C of the 146th Field Artillery, 41st Division. This group was one of the early transports to France.

Private Wisthoff was wounded on July 28, 1918, most likely at the Battle of Chateau Thierry. He died the following day. His body eventually was returned to Lodi, and he was buried in Lodi Memorial Cemetery.

JOSEPH GEORGE CAMPODONICO

Private – Company E, 47th Infantry, 4th Division

Joseph was born February 8, 1893, on Copperopolis Road, just east of Stockton. His parents were Emanuel and Louisa, both immigrants from Italy. In the 1900 Census, the family was living in Waterloo; and in 1910, they lived on Copperopolis Road. By 1920, the family had moved into the city and resided on O Street. On his draft registration in 1917, Joseph stated that he was a self-employed merchant. In the 1912 voter registration, he wrote that he was a farmer.

Joseph enlisted on November 15, 1917, and was sent to Camp Lewis, Washington, for training. He was assigned to Company E of the 47th Infantry, 41st Division as a draft replacement.

Private Campodonico was killed by machine gun fire during one of the first battles of Chateau Thierry, France. He died August 8, 1918, and was buried in Chery on the banks of the Vesle River, with a French priest officiating. His body eventually was sent home to Stockton, and he was given a hero's burial in the San Joaquin Catholic Cemetery. At the time of his death, Joseph was the fifth young man from St. Gertrude's Parish to die in the war.

ADAM KLEIN

Private – Company A, 47th Infantry, 4th Division

Adam Klein was born November 17, 1891, in Stockton. His parents, Antone and Magdalin, and oldest brother George had emigrated from Germany in 1890. By the 1900 Census, the family was living in Waterloo, east of Stockton. In 1910, the Kleins resided at 492 Grove Street with their nine children. Interestingly, Adam had four other brothers who registered for the draft, but only Adam and his older brother Edwin joined the war effort. At the time of the draft in 1917, the family was living at 2140 E. Hazelton.

Private Klein was assigned to Company A, 47th Infantry in the 4th Division. On August 3, 1918, while manning the front line in their trench, he was shot in the back, and the bullet went through the chest. He was sent to the field hospital but was transferred to Base Hospital

No. 1. He died from his wounds on August 12, 1918. He was buried in the cemetery beside the hospital. Eventually, his body was shipped home, arriving in Stockton on June 3, 1921. He was buried in the San Joaquin County Catholic Cemetery with full honors.

VAUGHN J. KEIFER

Private – Company E, 37ᵗʰ Engineers

VAUGHN KEIFER

Vaughn was born in October 1881 in Nebraska. On September 16, 1906, Vaughn enlisted in the US Army. He served five years and was discharged at Fort Baker, California, on September 15, 1911. He was working as a lineman for the Army.

It appears that Vaughn's father followed him out to California as both are found in the 1916 City of Stockton Directory residing at 312 Ophir. Vaughn was working as a signalman for the Southern Pacific Railroad. Employment records show that he was hired on August 15, 1916, and was assigned to the Stockton Yard as a brakeman.

Vaughn re-enlisted in the Army and was assigned to the 37ᵗʰ Engineers, E Company (a railroad transportation regiment). He was chosen to be trained in tractor assembly by the International Harvester Company, owners of the Case Threshing Machine. The plan was for the tractors to be shipped in parts to France and assembled by a specialized group of soldiers. Vaughn is mentioned in the book *History of Company E 37ᵗʰ Engineers* by Herbert C. Brown. Vaughn's photo is also found in the book.

Vaughn's unit left Hoboken on June 30, 1918, on the ship *Mauretania*. Their company saw immediate action, taking on troop bombs that exploded above the ground and sprayed shrapnel in all directions.

Vaughn, and many others from E Company, were killed on August 19, 1918, most while sleeping in their pup tents.

Vaughn was buried at the Aisne-Marne American Cemetery in Belleau, France. He rests in Plot B, Row 1 - Grave 7.

WALTER ARTHUR BICKNELL

Private, Company C, 50ᵗʰ Battalion, Canadian Expeditionary Forces

Walter was born in San Francisco to John W. and Phebe (Morgan) Bicknell on January 3, 1898. His father was born in Canada. In 1900, the family resided in the Castoria Township, between French Camp and Manteca. Walter's aunt, Bertha Shinn, lived in Manteca and was most likely the reason the family had moved into the area. By 1910, the Bicknells were in San Jose, when Phebe died. Now widowed, John decided to move back to Didsbury, Alberta, a town near Red Deer where he owned a farm.

In 1916, Walter joined his father in Alberta and proceeded to enlist in the Canadian Expeditionary Forces. He was attached to the 137ᵗʰ Battalion and shipped overseas. His military service was disrupted by many health problems.

Upon his arrival in England in 1917, Private Bicknell was admitted to Raven's Croft Military Hospital for appendicitis. The hospital staff operated and sent him to the 2ⁿᵈ Eastern General

Hospital in Brighton for recovery. While there, his wound became gangrenous, which delayed his discharge until April 3.

Walter was readmitted to the hospital on August 13, 1917, after complaining of a severe headache. He had a fever of 102 and was diagnosed with influenza. While in recovery, it was discovered that he suffered from syphilis. So, he was transferred on August 23 to the Trafford Hall Red Cross Hospital in Manchester, England. After treatment, he was discharged on October 5, 1917. He signed his last will and testament on October 16, 1917, leaving everything to his father. Walter was then assigned to C Company of the 50ᵗʰ Battalion.

Walter's company was sent to France, but Walter was kept in England to make sure he was fully recovered. He finally received orders to leave for France in April 1918. He rejoined his company now involved in heavy fighting along the Western Front.

On September 2, 1918, his company was crossing the Hindenburg line at Dury. Private Bicknell suffered a gunshot wound to his abdomen. He died two days later, on September 4, 1918. He was buried in the Ligny-St Flochel British Cemetery in Pas de Calais, France. He now rests in Section 111 - Grave E19.

LOUIS LAFARQUE

Fireman 3rd Class - United States Navy

Louis LaFarque was born in 1897 in San Francisco to French immigrants Jean and Madeline LaFarque. In 1910, the family moved to San Rafael and later moved to Vallejo. Louis and his brother John Albert grew up near Mare Island, where his parents owned a laundry service.

In 1917, John had moved to Pasadena for a job as a painter. John joined the Naval Reserve and was sent to England on the USS New Mexico. Louis soon followed in his brother's footsteps. He went to Mare Island to enlist. Soon after the enlistment, his father found work in Stockton with the City Parks Department. Jean and Madeline moved to 124 W. Worth Street.

Louis was assigned to the armored cruiser *USS San Diego*. On July 19, 1918, the ship experienced an explosion off the coast of New York and sank. The cause of the explosion is still unsolved today. Louis was thrown into the water, and he managed to stay afloat for three hours, until he was seen and rescued.

He then was assigned to the *USS Mt. Vernon*, a transport ship that was originally a German cruise ship. At the beginning of the war, it sailed into New York Harbor and was seized by the US Government and turned over to the US Navy. Louis made eight crossings aboard the Mt. Vernon. But on September 5, 1918, while heading back to the United States, the ship was torpedoed by a German U-boat off the coast of France. Notes from the ship state, "Vessel struck by one torpedo starboard side flooding #4 Fireroom." Thirty-six men were killed, including Fireman Third Class Louis LaFarque.

Louis was buried at the Cypress Hills National Cemetery in Brooklyn, New York. His parents remained in Stockton, but his mother never recovered from his death. She spent time in Stockton State Hospital, most likely from effects of depression. Jean died sometime before 1947. Madeline eventually moved to Santa Rosa. Louis' brother

John remained in Stockton and died in 1960. He is buried in Golden Gate National Cemetery in San Bruno.

CLYDE RAYMOND STAMPER

Corporal – Supply Company, 162nd Infantry, 41st Division

Corporal - Company G, 18th Infantry, 1st Division

Clyde was born in Lockeford, to Hosea and Annie Stamper on April 10, 1896.The family resided there until 1907, when Hosea died. Annie, who was a dressmaker, found work in San Francisco. In the 1910 Census, she lived on Geary Street with her daughter Lynne and son Clyde. During the 1917 draft registration, Clyde had moved back to Lockeford. He was working as a farm laborer for the Locke Company. He must have been one of the early enlistees, as he was on the ship *Susquehanna* being transported to France on December 12, 1917. At the time, Clyde was a wagoner serving in the Supply Company, 162nd Infantry of the 41st Division. He later requested a transfer to a different unit, along with James Miller.

Clyde was killed in action during the battle of St. Mihiel on September 12, 1918. He was buried at the St. Mihiel American Cemetery in Thiaucourt, France, in Section 18, Plot 2 - Grave 104. His records state that he was a Corporal in Company G, 18th Infantry, of the 1st Division.

Years later, Clyde's sister requested that his body be exhumed and transferred to the San Francisco National Cemetery. His final resting place is in Plot A – Grave 117.

FRANCIS "FRANK" ROBERT PATNOE

Private – 49th Engineers

Frank was born to Louis and Ellen (Crofton) Patnoe on June 19, 1892, in Rawlings, Wyoming (although in 1917, he stated he was born in Desoto, Nebraska). He was one of six children. Sometime before 1914, the family moved to Portland, Oregon, where his mother died on Christmas Day, 1914.

By 1916, Frank was working as a brakeman for the Northern Pacific Railroad in Portland. Unfortunately, he lost his job in January 1917. He and a friend stole some liquor from a railcar and were found inebriated in their hotel room. So, the company fined him $6.00 and asked for his resignation.

In February 1917, Frank travelled to St. Paul, Minnesota, to apply for a job with the local railway. He most likely did not get the job, since the company did not make any inquiry with the Northern Pacific. So, in June 1917, when he completed his draft registration card, Frank was working as a trainman for the Whitehall Estate Company and lived in Tracy, California.

Due to his experience with the railroad, Frank was assigned to the Railway Maintenance of Equipment Division, Company B of the 49th Engineers. Private Patnoe was transported with his company on the ship *France* on July 9, 1918. His next of kin was his sister Mable, who lived in Vancouver, Washington.

Private Patnoe was killed in action during the battle of St. Mihiel on September 15, 1918. It was the final day of this battle, which involved the French and American forces under the command of General John J. Pershing. It was one of the first major tank and air attacks led by the American Expeditionary Forces. The ground was muddy, sometimes knee deep. Provisions could not be moved and were left along the way as the Allies advanced. Frank was part of the company responsible for this equipment, and he most likely fell while attempting to save supplies.

He was buried in a temporary grave. Later, Private Patnoe was interred in the St. Mihiel American Cemetery in Thiaucourt, France. He rests in Plot A, Row 22 - Grave 28.

HAROLD ARLO SEXTON

Corporal – Company L, 363rd Infantry, 91st Division

Harold was born in Rio, Illinois, to Oscar and Mary Sexton on August 16, 1894. The family moved to Eugene, Oregon, where Oscar got a job as a retail merchant. Harold attended local schools and was a graduate of the University of Oregon.

In 1915, he moved to Stockton with his sister Velma. He was hired as a clerk and accountant for the freight office of the Southern Pacific Railroad. His 1917 draft registration stated that he lived at 807 N. El Dorado. He enlisted and became one the 22 young men making up the first Stockton contingency that left for Camp Lewis on September 9, 1917. His parents decided to move to Stockton sometime before Harold left for Washington. Oscar took a job at Holt Manufacturing to be nearer his children.

Harold did not pass his physical at Camp Lewis and was rejected for service. Undeterred, he underwent two surgeries and spent three months in the hospital before being accepted. He was given the rank of Corporal and placed in one of the four Honor Companies that were given a tour of Canada on their way to the East Coast for deployment. Also serving in Company L was Herbert Adams, another Stockton lad. The company left for France in July 1918.

Harold was killed in action on September 20, 1918, near Verdun, France, just prior to the Final Offensive in the Meuse-Argonne. His parents chose to have him buried at the Meuse-Argonne National Cemetery in Romagne, France. His body was laid to rest in Plot A, Row 43 - Grave 21.

DARRELL COLLINS MITCHELL

Private – 44th Balloon Company, Aviation Section, Signal Corps

Darrell Mitchell was born in Porterville on July 8, 1890, to James Joseph and Emmaline Mitchell. In 1900, the family resided in rural Kern County; and in the 1910 Census, they had moved to rural Fresno County.

In completing his draft registration in 1917, Darrell stated that he operated a harvester for the San Joaquin Valley Farm Land Company.

Darrell joined the Aero Service and was assigned to the 44th Balloon Company. He was transported with his company to France on the ship *Charles* on July 10, 1918. Balloon companies were being used for reconnaissance, including photographs of the enemy position. He was killed in action on September 24, 1918, while serving in the Oise-Aisne campaign.

Private Darrell C Mitchell was buried in the Oise-Aisne American Cemetery at Fere-en-Tardenois, France, in Plot C, Row 7 - Grave 22.

HAROLD EDWARD CARY

Corporal – 363rd Infantry, 91st Division

Harold was born in Lodi on August 26, 1895, to Edward and Anna Cary. His father was a rancher and a contractor. He also owned the Lodi Waterworks and Electrical Company. In the 1910 Census, the family resided on West Elm Street in Lodi. When Harold registered to vote in 1916, he was living at 115 N. School Street.

Harold's parents divorced, and his mother moved to San Francisco. Sometime following his voter registration, Harold moved to San Francisco to be with his mother. On June 5, 1917, when he completed his draft card, Harold lived at 150 Post Street and was a clerk for the hardware store Dunham, Carrigan and Hayden.

Harold entered military service October 6, 1917, and was sent to Camp Lewis, Washington. He was assigned to the 363rd Infantry Regiment in the 91st Division. This regiment, dubbed "San Francisco's Own," was filled with men from the City and from San Joaquin County. The regiment arrived in France in July 1918 after extensive training. Harold was promoted to Corporal and proved himself a fine leader who gained the respect of the men.

Commanded by General John "Black Jack" Pershing, the 91st Division took the lead in the Meuse-Argonne Forest battles of the Final Offensive (September 26 through November 11). While guiding his company through barbed wire, Harold was killed by a sniper on the first day of the campaign, September 26, 1918. He was buried near where he fell at Bois de Cheppy. Eventually, his family chose to have his body relocated to the Meuse-Argonne American Cemetery in Romagne, France. He lies in Plot B, Row 32 - Grave 12.

EDMUND THOMAS KASPER

Private – Headquarters Company, 363rd Infantry, 91st Division

Edmund was a native Stocktonian, born on January 7, 1895, to Matthias Joseph and Matilda Kasper. Matthias was a butcher, and Edmund soon joined his father in that profession. But by the 1917 draft registration, Edmund was working as a farmhand for Mrs. Mabel Ladd.

Edmund was sent to Camp Lewis and assigned to the 91st Division, 363rd Infantry. While in training, he took first honors in shooting and was considered the third best shot in the entire 91st Division. With his marksmanship, he was assigned to the Headquarters Company.

The unit shipped off to France on July 6, 1918, and almost immediately saw action. Edmund was in France but a few short months. He was killed in action on September 26, 1918, during the first day of the massive offensive of the Meuse Argonne. The 91st had been given the task of leading the front line, and Edmund fell during the first few hours.

His body was sent back to Stockton and laid to rest in the San Joaquin Catholic Cemetery.

MARTIN TROY, JR.

Private – Company M, 47ᵗʰ Infantry, 4ᵗʰ Division

Martin was born in Lodi on March 26, 1892, to Martin and Mary Troy. In the 1900 Census, the family lived in Woodbridge. In 1910, they lived in Elkhorn Township, and Martin Jr. stated that he was a farm laborer.

By the 1917 draft registration, Martin was working for Frey Farms and the family had moved to South School Street in Lodi. Martin had three brothers; William, Frank and Reuben. Frank and William also joined the military, and William was assigned to a unit in Siberia while Frank was stationed at Camp Kearny.

Martin was sent to Camp Lewis and later selected in the replacement draft and sent to Camp Greene, North Carolina. He was attached to Company M of the 47ᵗʰ Infantry, 4ᵗʰ Division.

Private Troy was killed in action on September 26, 1918, the first day of the 100 Day Offensive in the Argonne Forest. It is noted on *Find-a-Grave* that his body was either lost or destroyed, so he was not buried in a cemetery. It is quite likely that his body was buried with the hundreds of other young men who gave their lives on the first day of the charge to go "over the top" and push the German Army out of France.

JERROLD JOSEPH AGGELER

Corporal – Headquarters Company, Company C,
363rd Infantry, 91st Division

Jerrold was born in Ferndale, Humboldt County, on March 18, 1891, to Joseph and Jennie Amelia (Bailey) Aggeler. The family owned a dairy near Grizzly Bluff. In 1908, Joseph moved his family to Roberts Island, just west of Stockton. He purchased a large farm, which he owned for many years.

Jerrold grew up working on the family farm. He also ran a dredge on Roberts Island and was a member of First Presbyterian Church in Stockton. He was liked by all who met him.

Jerrold enlisted in September 1917 and was sent to Camp Lewis. He was assigned to the Headquarters Company of the 363rd Infantry, 91st Division. He shipped overseas with his unit in July 1918.

Once in France, Corporal Aggeler requested a transfer to Company C, which enabled him to join the fighting. His last letter home was written on September 25. He died on the second day of the Meuse-Argonne Offensive on September 27, 1918, as his company went "over the top." Military records state he was killed in action by a sniper's bullet. He was survived by his parents and his brother, Bailey.

Jerrold's body eventually was shipped back to his parents, and he was buried in Parkview Cemetery. When his parents and brother died, they were laid to rest next to him

JOHN GHRIST ANDERSON

Private – 6th Field Artillery, 1st Division

John was born on June 23, 1895, in Highlands, North Carolina. His parents were William H and Susannah "Sudie" (Brown) Anderson. They had 11 children. When William died in 1912, Sudie moved her family to California and settled in Lodi. The family resided at 418 W. Pine Street.

In the 1917 draft registration, John had moved to Los Angeles and worked as a shoe salesman for the PE Woods Children's Shoe Store on Broadway. He lived on South Figueroa Street. He joined the California National Guard and was in Battery D of the 144th Field Artillery. John enlisted from Los Angeles but gave his Lodi address as his home.

Because of his enlistment in the National Guard, John was soon attached to the United States Army's 6th Field Artillery, 1st Division.

Private Anderson fought with his division in some very difficult battles. The 1st provided back-up to the British, Australians and Canadians in the Battle of Amiens. Next, they were participants in the Battle of Somme and followed 10 days later with the Battle of St. Mihiel. After another 10- day rest, the 1st Division fought valiantly in the Meuse-Argonne Campaign.

Anderson fell to enemy fire on the second day of the Meuse-Argonne on September 27, 1918. He was buried near the town of Souilly. His body was later disinterred and laid to rest in the Meuse-Argonne American Cemetery. He now rests in Plot F, Row 28, - Grave 32.

CHARLES D. FONTANELLA

Private - Machine Gun Company, 39th Infantry, 4th Division

Charles was born February 1, 1885, in Stockton. Charles grew up on West Lane and worked for his father's gardening company. He was an early enlistee, joining in September 1917. He trained at Camp Lewis, but he eventually was sent to Camp Mills. Due to his height (he was over six feet), he was assigned to the 39th Infantry's Machine Gun Company, 4th Division.

His unit fought in some of the early battles of the campaign in France. He was the Fontanellas' only son, and his mother had expressed the fear that he would not return home. Private Fontanella was killed on September 27, 1918, while fighting in the Argonne. His body was shipped home, and he was buried in San Joaquin Catholic Cemetery.

CARL ROBERT BERTEL GUSTAFSON

Sergeant – Company L, 363rd Infantry, 91st Division

Carl was born in Norkoping, Sweden, on April 20, 1893, to Johan and Amalia (Edmund) Gustafson. The family immigrated to the United States when Carl was three months old. Johan had a job in Ishpeming, Marquette County, Michigan. In 1900, the entire family was in Ishpeming, including Edith, who was born in Michigan in 1895.

In 1912, Johan died in Escalon. When Carl completed his draft card in 1917, he lived in Escalon, worked as a farmer and was the sole support of his widowed mother. Carl must have enlisted, since he would have been exempt. He joined enlistees at Camp Lewis for training and earned the rank of Sergeant.

Carl was on the *Benalla* when it left Hoboken on July 7, 1918. The manifest stated he was not yet assigned to a company. But he was included with the others from Company L of the 363rd Infantry.

Sergeant Gustafson lost his life during the Meuse-Argonne offensive on September 27, 1918. He was face-to-face with the enemy with bayonets drawn. He was buried near where he fell, and later his mother chose to have him laid to rest in the Meuse-Argonne American Cemetery. He now lies in Plot D, Row 13 - Grave 31.

Later, the Escalon American Legion would be named in his honor, along with fellow local soldier Cecil Thompson (Gustafson-Thompson Post 263).

EDWARD HANS LORENSEN

Corporal – Company "I, 363rd Infantry, 91st Division

Edward was listed in the *Soldiers of the Great War, Vol. 1,* pg. 18, as hailing from Santa Cruz County. He was the city editor of the Watsonville newspaper *Pajaronian*. His mother lived in Escalon, and she was listed as his next of kin, so his military records considered Escalon his hometown.

Edward was born on March 13, 1889, in San Francisco and at the time of his draft registration resided at 210 E. 5th Street in Watsonville. He stated he was married to his wife, Kathryn, and had served three months as a Sergeant in the California National Guard.

Edward was sent to Camp Lewis along with so many young men from Northern California. He earned the rank of Corporal and was assigned to Company "I" of the 363rd Infantry, 91st Division.

He was killed in action on September 27, 1918, in the Meuse-Argonne campaign. He was buried at the Meuse-Argonne American Cemetery in Romagne, France, in Plot D, Row 14 - Grave 7. His mother participated in the Mother's Pilgrimage of 1931, visiting his grave as a guest of the United States Government.

JAMES GARDNER MCDERMOTT

Private – Company M, 362nd Infantry, 91st Division

James was born on February 5, 1893, in San Francisco to Lawrence and Mary (Gardner) McDermott. James was the fourth of six sons born to the couple. His grandfather was a pioneer who helped settle the Livermore area. In the 1910 Census, the McDermott family was living in the Tulare Township west of Tracy in San Joaquin County. Lawrence worked at the Carnegie Brick plant in the Corral Hollow area along Tesla Road. This area was known for its coal deposits. In the 1917 draft, James states that he is a miner for the Western Rock Product Company.

James was one of the Tracy men who comprised the San Joaquin contingency that departed for Camp Lewis on December 14, 1917. He was assigned to Company M of the 362 Infantry of the 91st Division. His unit sailed for France in July 1918.

While fighting in the Meuse-Argonne campaign, Private McDermott was killed in action on September 27, 1918. He was the first young man from the Tracy area to die. His obituary mentioned that his brothers George and Frank also were serving in the war, both being with the 319th Engineers.

James's body eventually was sent back to Tracy, and he was buried at the Tracy Public Cemetery. The Tracy American Legion Post 172 was named in his honor.

HENRY ARNE THORSON

Private – 363rd Infantry, 91st Division

Henry was from Modesto, but his sister, JB Wott, was his next of kin. She resided in Stockton, so the United States Army listed Henry as being one of Stockton's native sons.

Private Thorson was killed in action on September 27, 1918, on the second day of the 100 Day Offensive as he went "over the top" at the Cote Dame Mare hill. He was buried in the Meuse-Argonne American Cemetery in Romagne, France. His final resting place is in Plot D, Row 17 - Grave 9.

WILLIAM E. STONE

Private – Company M, 363rd Infantry, 91st Division.

William Stone was born in Springdale, Arkansas, on September 20, 1886. His parents are not known. In the 1900 Census, William and his three siblings lived with his brother, Dudley, and his wife, Tulah, and their two sons, Jesse and Alan.

In the 1908 Stockton City Directory, William worked as a fireman at Stockton State Hospital and resided at 7 S. Center. By 1909, he had been promoted to engineer, which was noted in the 1910 Census.

When William completed the 1917 draft, he no longer worked at the State Hospital. He was a farmer with Garfield Stone (most likely a relative) on Victoria Island.

William's nephew Alan had enlisted in the Marine Corps just 21 days after the United States entered the war. He was killed in April 1918, the second death from Stockton. Upon learning of his nephew's death, William enlisted in the Army. He was sent to Camp Lewis and assigned to Company M of the 363rd Infantry, 91st Division.

Private Stone was killed in action on September 28, 1918, on the third day of the Meuse-Argonne Offensive. His body was later returned to the family, and he was buried in the family plot in Hubberton Cemetery, Arkansas.

LESTER LLOYD WEYLANDT

Corporal – Company K, 363rd Infantry, 91st Division

Lester was born to Alfred and Maggie Weylandt on November 28, 1895, in Pasadena. In 1900, the Weylandts were living in Everett, Washington. In 1910, the family was residing on Copperopolis Road, Douglass Township, near the town of Peters in San Joaquin County. By this time, Lester had five siblings. According to an article in *The Stockton Record*, the Weylants had moved to the Peters area in 1908.

Lester's 1917 draft registration has him living with his parents and working as a farm laborer for D. W. Miller. He was engaged to Miss Amalia V. Scheffel, also of Peters.

Lester left for Camp Lewis with one of the early contingencies from San Joaquin County, leaving Stockton on September 17, 1917. He spent nine months in training and was considered an exemplary soldier. He earned the rank of Corporal and was attached to Company K of the 363rd Infantry, 91st Division. He was one of the young men chosen to tour Canada prior to being transported to France as a reward for his work ethic in camp.

Corporal Weylandt was in the front line of the Meuse-Argonne Offensive and was killed instantly by an exploding shell on September 29, 1918. His body was buried near where he fell in the small town of Eclais-Fountaine, France.

Lester's body eventually was exhumed and returned to his parents in 1921. They gave him a final resting place in the Parkview Cemetery in Manteca alongside so many other young men from the area who had made the ultimate sacrifice.

RALPH WILLIAM GILLESPIE

Sergeant – Company G, 363rd Infantry, 91st Division

Ralph was born to William Wallace and Mary Anna Gillespie on their ranch three miles east of Lodi on June 17, 1894. He had two older brothers, George and Howard, and three sisters, Mable, Nelle and Edna.

On his 1917 draft registration, Ralph stated he worked on the family farm. He was part of the second San Joaquin County contingency that left Stockton on September 17, 1917, for Camp Lewis. At camp, Ralph showed himself to be an exemplary soldier. Within two weeks, he had earned the rank of Corporal. He was attached to Company G of the 363rd Infantry, 91st Division. After eight months of training, his company shipped out of Philadelphia aboard the ship *City of Cairo* on July 6, 1918. Upon arriving in France, Ralph was promoted to Sergeant.

Sergeant Ralph Gillespie was considered a model soldier. His friend, Sergeant H. R. DeGiegorio, wrote to Ralph's mother, telling her of his sunny disposition: always positive and always with a smile. Ralph wrote many letters home while in the fight. He told family that he had spent two months at the front. Sgt. DeGiegorio was with Ralph in the Meuse-Argonne battle as they went "over the top." He told Ralph's family that he died instantly on September 30, 1918.

Ralph's body was sent home to Lodi, and he was buried in Lodi Memorial Cemetery, Pioneer I. His parents received a certificate from the Adjunct General's office, dated January 4, 1919, that Sergeant Ralph Gillespie "died with honor in the service of his country."

JAMES HERBERT MEAD

Corporal – 363rd Infantry, 91st Division

James H. Mead was born in Oakland on February 14, 1893, to James William and Alvida Mead. His father was a locomotive engineer, but he died suddenly in 1903. Alvida remarried in 1906 to John B. Woods. James had three siblings and two half-siblings.

His mother died in 1915, so he left home and took a job as a gas engineer for Wood's Irrigation and Drainage and lived on Roberts Island west of Stockton. He was part of the early contingency that left Stockton for Camp Lewis in September 1917.

On July 31, 1918, Corporal Mead left for France "unassigned" on the ship *Elpenor*. Also on board was another local young soldier, Hope McFall from Manteca.

Upon arrival, James was assigned to the 91st Division's 363rd Infantry. Corporal Mead was with the division as it made its charge to go "over the top." He was killed in action on September 30, 1918, in the Meuse-Argonne Offensive. He was buried near where he fell but was given his final resting place in Plot G, Row 27 - Grave 35 in the Meuse-Argonne American Cemetery in Romagne, France.

HOPE LAFAYETTE MCFALL

Sergeant – Company L, 363rd Infantry, 91st Division

Hope was born on July 29, 1892, in Louisville, Kentucky, to Russell and Nancy (Woods) McFall. By 1900, the McFall family had moved to Missouri, first living in Turnback until buying a farm in Marionville, where they grew grain.

On July 13, 1917, Hope married Norma Dempsey, and the couple moved to Manteca. Hope's oldest brother, John "Lucky" McFall, had moved to Manteca and owned a garage. Hope went to work for his brother.

Hope enlisted on September 19, 1917. He was in one of the first contingencies from San Joaquin County and was named Captain of their group. They arrived by train to Camp Lewis for training. Hope was promoted to Sergeant and assigned to Company L of the 363rd Infantry, 91st Division. The unit arrived in France in July 1918.

Sergeant McFall led his company into the Argonne Forest during the first days of the Meuse-Argonne Offensive. He was killed in action on October 1, 1918, and was buried near where he fell. His body eventually was returned to the states, and his mother requested that his body be sent to Marionville. He is buried in the Marionville IOOF Cemetery. Lucky named his firstborn daughter Hope in honor of his brother. American Legion Post 249 in Manteca is named in his honor.

Hope and Norma's son, John Joseph McFall, was born February 20, 1918. Hope never got to see his son. John was raised by his maternal grandparents, Joseph and Margarita Dempsey, on their farm in Manteca. He became very successful. He attended UC Berkeley and served in the Security Intelligence Corps during World War II. He earned his law degree and after the war was elected Mayor of Manteca. He led a life of public service, serving as a California State Assemblyman and later served 11 terms in the United States Congress. For a time, he served as majority whip. He retired in 1978 and moved to Virginia, where he died at the age of 88.

CECIL EARL THOMPSON

Private - Company K, 364th Infantry, 91st Division

Cecil was born May 4, 1896, in Sacramento, to Charles and Stella. He had two older brothers and a younger sister. In 1900, Charles was a farmer in the Cosumnes area of Sacramento County. In 1910, the family had moved to Turlock in Stanislaus County, where Charles was a teamster. By 1917, the family lived in Escalon.

In the 1917 draft, Cecil was living in the small town of Fellows in Kern County. Fellows, just northwest of Taft, had become a boomtown with the discovery of the Midway Gusher in 1909. Today, the area is the third largest oilfield on US soil. Cecil was working in the oilfields for the CC Motor Company.

Thompson was drafted while working in Kern County. He was in the first draft contingent that left Bakersfield in September 1917. He was sent by train to Camp Lewis, where he met up with many of his San Joaquin County friends.

Private Thompson was transported on the ship *Olympic* on July 12, 1918, with his fellow soldiers of Company K, 364th Infantry, 91st Division. His division participated in both the St. Mihiel and Meuse-Argonne campaigns.

On September 28, 1918, just two days into the fighting in the Argonne Forest near Eclisfontaine, France, he was given scouting duty. *"Private Thompson went forward on his own initiative and located the position of the enemy on our front. After an all-night exploit, he returned with this information. Without rest, he went out in the morning, and located a troublesome machine-gun nest."* For this act, he was recommended for the Distinguished Service Cross for extraordinary heroism in action.

Tragically, the medal was to be given posthumously. Just two days later, on October 1, 1918, Private Thompson was killed in the line of duty. His body eventually was sent to Escalon, and he was given a hero's funeral and buried in Parkview Cemetery in Manteca.

The Escalon American Legion is named in his honor (Gustafson-Thompson Post 263).

NB: The quotation was taken from the actual account submitted by his superior officer for consideration of an official citation. The American Government determined he met the criteria of "exceptional heroism and conspicuous service above and beyond the call of duty."

WILLIAM IRVING TREDWAY

Sergeant – Company B, 363rd Infantry, 91st Division

Will was born in Glenbrook, Lake County, California on July 2, 1896, to Orvis and Sadie Tredway. His parents divorced when Will was young, and he lived with his father on the Tredway Ranch just west of Lodi. In the 1910 US Census, his father had been married five years to his second wife and resided in the Elkhorn Township of San Joaquin County.

By the 1917 draft registration, Will was living in Lodi and was a farm laborer for E. J. Miller farms in Dunnigan, Yolo County. Later that year, he moved back to Glenwood to be with his mother. Will was drafted and sent to Camp Lewis. Before shipping out, he married Ruby Blann on April 6, 1918, in Pierce County Washington.

He was transported on July 6, 1918, on the ship *Briton*. Will was promoted to Sergeant and assigned to Company B, 363rd Infantry of the 91st Division. This division faced heavy odds during the battle of the Meuse-Argonne, which began on September 26, 1918. Will was wounded in the early days of the battle. He succumbed to his injuries on October 1, 1918.

Sergeant Tredway was laid to rest in the Meuse-Argonne American Cemetery in Romagne, Lorraine, France; Plot B, Row 25 - Grave 15. Sadie was on the Mother's Pilgrimage list for 1930-33, so she most likely traveled to Paris and was given the opportunity to say her final goodbye at her son's grave. She was the only one from Lake County on the list.

CHARLES ERIC WALTHER

Corporal – Company N, 109th Infantry, 28th Division

Charles Walther was born in Sacramento on January 21, 1890, to Charles Frederick and Florence "Lena" (Dinkelspiel) Walther. The family lived in Liberty Township north of Lodi. Charles graduated from the College of the Pacific in San Jose, being a fine violinist.

In the 1917 draft registration, Charles was living in San Mateo and worked at Redwood City High School as a music teacher. When he was drafted, he told friends that he would take up the cause and learn to be a good soldier. He shared his belief that he would not return home alive.

While at Camp Kearny, Private Walther was true to his word. He became an expert marksman and was chosen to depart with Company 15 on June 28, 1918, as part of the Automatic Replacement Draft.

Upon arrival in France, he was attached to Company N, 109th Infantry of the 28th Division, earning the rank of Corporal. His unit fought in some of the major battles: Chateau Thierry, Marne-Aisne, and the Oise-Aisne. It was there that he was burned with mustard gas and sent to the hospital in Courmont.

While recovering, the hospital building was bombed, and he suffered further wounds. Not fully healed, he joined his company at the front with General Pershing in the Argonne Forest. He went "over the top" on September 26, 1918. Within 48 hours, his company had no officers alive. He kept advancing for six more days, when he finally fell. Corporal Walther was so far out in front that his body was not found by the burying squad.

Finally, on October 4, 1918, he was discovered by men of the 128th Field Artillery. He lay upward with his New Testament open on his chest. He had pressed flowers from the French fields in the book, which lay strewn across his body. He was buried in France and eventually sent home to his parents in 1921. His final resting place is in the Elk Grove-Cosumnes Cemetery. A touching tribute was written by the librarian of College of the Pacific providing details of his heroism.

EARL WOODWARD

Corporal – Machine Gun Company, 363rd Infantry, 91st Division

Earl was born on October 19, 1889, in Oakland, California, to Samuel Gideon and Aline Woodward. In 1900, the Woodwards were residing in Azusa, Los Angeles County; and by the 1910 Census, they had moved to Newman near Crows Landing in Stanislaus County.

In 1917 on his draft registration card, Earl stated that he was working on the family farm on Durham Ferry Road in Lathrop, California. He was 27 years old and had two brothers and two sisters.

Earl went with one of the early contingencies to Camp Lewis. He was assigned to the Machine Gun Company of the 363rd Infantry, 91st Division. He was transported on the ship *Benalla* with so many other local young soldiers of the 363rd.

While fighting in the Meuse-Argonne Offensive, Corporal Woodward had gained an advanced position. He and another soldier occupied a shell hole for the night, acting as guards for their company.

Early on the morning of October 1, 1918, he was spotted by a German sharpshooter. He was killed instantly with a bullet to his head. He died the same day as Hope McFall, another soldier from the Manteca area. Corporal Woodward was buried at the Meuse-Argonne American Cemetery in Romagne, France, in Plot H, Row 43 - Grave 9.

FRANK WILLIAM ELSHOLZ

Private –Machine Gun Company, 363rd Infantry, 91st Division

Frank was born in Galt, California, on December 27, 1888. He worked on his family farm near Elk Grove. But in 1916, Frank moved to Stockton with his sister Gussie. He first lived at 548 E. Sonora, then moved to 25 S. El Dorado. He was employed as a chauffeur/driver.

Frank was drafted and sent with the first contingency from San Joaquin County along with Karl Ross, Harold Sexton and Herbert Adams. Twenty-two young men from Stockton were sent to Camp Lewis, Washington, for training. Frank was assigned to the Machine Gun Company, 363rd Infantry of the 91st Wild West Division. The 91st was transported on the ship *Benalla* on July 7, 1918, from Hoboken, New Jersey, and landed in France days later.

By early October, the 363rd Infantry had been involved in many significant battles, including the St. Mihiel Offensive (September 1918) and the Meuse-Argonne Offensive (September, October). Private Elsholz succumbed to wounds inflicted in the Argonne Forest. He was buried in the Meuse-Argonne American Cemetery, Plot B, Row 34 - Grave 18. His surviving relative, Gussie Thein, who lived at 1232 S. California Street, Stockton, was notified of his death.

PAUL RAPHAEL HOLDZKOM

Corporal – Machine Gun Company C, 363rd Infantry, 91st Division

Paul was born on April 5, 1895, in San Bernardino, California, to Allen and Ida (Mattock) Holdzkom and was their only son. He was living in Imperial at the time of the draft, so he became part of the first contingency sent from that county to Camp Lewis.

Paul's connection with Stockton came in many ways. First, he was an agent for the Holt Manufacturing Company and spent time in Stockton learning about the Caterpillar tractor he was selling. When he got to Camp Lewis, he was placed in the same Machine Gun Company as Karl Ross and Frank Elsholz, also from Stockton. All three young men were shipped out together on the ship *Benalla* on July 7. 1918. They fought together as a band of brothers, and all gave their lives for the noble cause.

Paul was killed in action in the Argonne Forest during the battle on October 2, 1918. He was eventually sent back to San Bernardino and buried in Mountain View Cemetery. He was a member of the Morning Star Lodge, so the local Masons were put in charge of his service.

PHILIP W. SHERLOCK

Wagoner – Company H, 58th Infantry, 4th Division

Philip was born on November 4, 1889, in New York City. He and his brother Walter arrived in Stockton prior to 1916. Philip worked for J. M Bigger, a farmer in Holt who was also a County Administrator. In the 1917 draft, Philip was living on Cherokee Lane north of Stockton. He and his brother had purchased a small farm.

But Philip was drafted, being one of the first in Stockton. The brothers realized they could not keep the farm under operation, so they sold the land. Walter moved into town to work at the pencil factory while Philip was sent to basic training in Washington at either Camp Lewis or the Vancouver Barracks.

Sometime during his time at camp, Philip was assigned to the 4th Division and sent to Camp Greene in North Carolina. The 4th had been created in November 1917 with troops who were training in Monterey, the Vancouver Barracks and Camp Greene. Later, it was filled with replacements from Camp Lewis and other training camps. Philip was most likely one of the young men drafted as a replacement. He was attached to Company H, 58th Infantry.

Private Sherlock's company shipped out on May 7, 1918. They were transported on the *Rhesus* out of Philadelphia. When they arrived in France, the division was assigned extra training. From May 18 to June 10, they trained with the British in Picardy; and from June 11 to July 17, they trained with the French Sixth Army at Meaux. During this training, Philip was assigned as a wagoner, so he must have had experience with horses.

On July 18, the 4th Division was sent into battle during the Aisne-Marne operation, which lasted until July 22. The 58th was instrumental in the capture of the town of Chevillon. They continued in battle from July 28 to August 6, now focused on the area near Chateau-Thierry and the Vesle River. The units merged near Champagne, and the 4th Division now occupied the entire Vesle Sector.

After a three-week rest, Philip and the entire 4th Division were sent to St. Mihiel. Again, they were heavily involved in the fight. As a wagoner, Philip was responsible for the well-being of the horses, crucially necessary to transport ammunition and supplies. After four days of fighting, the 4th was moved again; this time to the Meuse-Argonne.

The 7th Infantry Brigade, which included the 58th, took a lead in the September 26, 1918, attack. They captured the towns of Cuisy and Septsarges. It was there that Wagoner Philip Sherlock met his death. He was killed in action on October 2, 1918, as his company was holding the line. Their relief did not arrive until October 5.

Philip was buried in an area near where he died. In 1921, his family was given the choice to have his body sent home or be buried in one of the newly created American cemeteries. His mother, Mary, requested that Wagoner Sherlock be laid to rest in the Meuse-Argonne American Cemetery in Romagne, France. He now rests in Plot C, Row 35 - Grave 1.

BERNARD JAMES IRWIN

Private/Bugler – Company G,
2nd Ammunition Train, Bugler Corps

Barney, or Jay as he was sometimes called, was born March 31, 1896, in Ocanto, Nebraska, to Mary and Dallas Irwin. The family moved to Stockton sometime before 1913. The Stockton City Directory of that year states the family resided at 1447 E. Main. According to an article in *The Stockton Record* in 1918, the family was building a home on the Smith Canal near Tuxedo Park. But in the 1920 Census, they were living on West Lane, apparently having fallen on hard times.

Bernard was musical and upon enlistment was assigned as a bugler for Company G, 2nd Ammunition Train. Few details were given as to

Bernard's death. He was killed in action on October 3, 1918, in the Meuse-Argonne Offensive. His body was buried in France; but in 1921, the family requested that his body be sent to Boise, Idaho. He was buried alongside his mother and his brother Patrick.

HERBERT HAROLD ADAMS

Corporal – Company L, 363ʳᵈ Infantry, 91ˢᵗ Division – Post Office Corps

Herbert was born March 2, 1894, in LaGrange, Tuolumne County, California, to William and Sarah Jane Adams. He was a graduate of Heald's Business College in Stockton and lived with his parents at 1236 E. Channel Street. In the 1913 Stockton City Directory, Herbert is working as the division manager of the Oro Electric Company. He then worked for a year as a stenographer for Stockton Iron Works. When he completed his draft registration in June 1917, Herbert was a shipping clerk for Sears & Roebuck.

Herbert volunteered to be part of the first contingent of young men to represent Stockton. The group of 22 left for Camp Lewis on September 9, 1917, with a patriotic send-off from the city's inhabitants.

Herbert was assigned to the Post Office Corps, Company L, 363ʳᵈ Infantry, 91ˢᵗ Division, earning the rank of Corporal. Another Stockton soldier, Harold A Sexton, was in this same company and was also part of the first contingent. Herbert's job as a mail carrier required him to run mail and other communications from headquarters to the frontline companies, often dodging shells and machine gun bullets.

On September 26, 1918, the 363ʳᵈ regiment was sent to the front line for the push through the Argonne Forest. Their assignment was to lead the division for nine straight days. Herbert fell on the last day of the drive on October 4, 1918. At the time, he was running mail and took cover in a hole with two other soldiers. A shell landed in the hole, killing the three men instantly. His body was sent back to Stockton, and he was buried in the Oakdale Citizens' Cemetery. He was a member of the Native Sons of the Golden West, Parlor 7, and belonged to the Yosemite Tent of the Knights of the Macabees. Both fraternal organizations participated in his burial.

JAMES BUDD ANDERSON

Private – Company D, 364ᵗʰ Infantry, 91ˢᵗ Division

James was born in Clements, California, on December 4, 1894, to Silas Franklin and Laura Agnes Anderson. He was named after the Governor of California James H. Budd, who hailed from Stockton.

The family lived in the Elliot Township of San Joaquin County in the town of Clements. In 1910, James attended Heald Business College in Stockton. After graduation, he was employed as a bookkeeper for Lodi Hardware Store. In 1912, he worked in the office of the Southern Pacific Railroad and later left its employ to take a job as a clerk for Chrisman & Clements. This business in Clements allowed him to work in his own hometown.

James was sent to Camp Lewis, where he was attached to Company D, 363th Infantry of the 91ˢᵗ Division. This group was transported on July 12, 1918, on the ship *Olympic.* They arrived in France in late July and prepared for battle.

Private Anderson was hit by shrapnel sometime in late September. He was sent to the hospital in Fleury, France, for treatment. He died of his wounds on October 4, 1918. He was buried in Fleury near Verdun, but his body was later transferred to the Meuse-Argonne American Cemetery in Romagne, France. He lies in Plot A, Row 31 - Grave 14

In 1920, the town of Clements dedicated a monument in his honor in the Glen View Cemetery.

GUY WALTER STAPLES

Corporal – Company H, 363rd Infantry, 91st Division

Guy was born to James and Lilly (Tull) Staples on February 16, 1896, in Stockton. He was one of nine children born to the couple. James owned a ranch in Douglas Township near the town of Linden. Lilly's father, T. Columbus Tull, was an early farmer in the Linden area.

In 1917, Guy stated on his draft form that he was working for G B McCauley Farms in Forest Lake, just north of Lodi. Guy enlisted and was sent to Camp Lewis. Prior to leaving for the East Coast, he was promoted to Private First Class and attached to Company H of the 363rd Infantry, 91st Division.

His company was sent to Philadelphia, where it was transported to France on July 6, 1918, aboard the ship *City of Cairo*. Upon arrival in France, the company was assigned to additional training. During that time, Guy was promoted to Corporal.

The 393rd was the integral point during the Meuse-Argonne Offensive. It took the lead as the 91st worked its way into the Argonne Forest. Corporal Staples' company made great advancements and pushed the Germans back several kilometers. But Guy was killed in action on October 4, 1918, the final day of the ten days of battle.

Corporal Staples' body was sent home, and he was buried in the Linden Cemetery.

LESLIE M. ROPER

Private – Company M, 141ˢᵗ Infantry, 36ᵗʰ Division

Leslie was born in 1898 to John H. and Elizabeth (Gregory) Roper in Texas. Leslie enlisted in 1917, having already been a soldier in the Texas National Guard. This Guard unit had been busy defending the Texas border from Mexican invasion (led by Pancho Villa). Leslie and his entire Guard militia were sent to Camp Bowie and assigned to Company M of the 141ˢᵗ Infantry, 36ᵗʰ Division.

Their unit began pulling out on July 6, 1918, after months of training. They arrived at Camp Mills in Brooklyn, New York, ready to serve. Private Roper was transported with his unit on July 26, 1918, on the ship *Finland*. Upon arrival, the 36ᵗʰ became part of the 71ˢᵗ Brigade and was assigned as a reserve for the French troops near the Marne River. Included was the AEF 2ⁿᵈ Division, which joined the French at St. Etienne, situated near Rheims (the Champagne District), France. They were under the command of Marine Major General John Lejeune.

The Brigade moved out on October 6. Since they were under the assumption that they were in reserve, they left behind many supplies. They had inadequate amounts of ammunition and grenades and could not move their mortar and 37 mm guns due to lack of draft animals. But they were being ordered to the front. By October 7, they had lost their guide, since the soldiers were strung out so far. Dauntless, they engaged the enemy on October 8, 1918.

On that first day of conflict, Private Leslie M. Roper was killed in action. His body was buried in a small town outside of Rheims.

After his death, Leslie's family decided to leave Texas and move to Stockton. His brother John had been hired by the Moore Equipment Company. In 1922, the United States government exhumed our soldiers from their temporary graves and were either transporting them home or burying them in the newly created American cemeteries in France and Belgium. By now, Private Roper's home address was Stockton, although he had never lived here.

His parents decided to have Leslie buried in the Meuse-Argonne American Cemetery in Romagne, France. His final rest is in Plot D, Row 24 - Grave 8.

CHARLES REUBEN CURRY

Bugler – Company D, 361st Infantry, 91st Division

Charles Curry was born in Ohio on August 4, 1894, to J. H. "Jay" Curry and Carrie Belle Gifford. The family moved to Stockton in 1902. By 1909, Jay and Carrie had divorced but remained in Stockton. Carrie resided at 1004 S. San Joaquin Street, and Jay lived at 127 E. Channel.

In the 1915 City Directory, Charles is working as a clerk for CP Rendon. He eventually was employed at the Eagle Drug Store on South Center Street and loved working the soda fountain. He was known by all who frequented the business.

Charles enlisted and was sent to Camp Lewis, where he was assigned as a bugler for Company D of the 361st Infantry, 91st Division. By this time, his mother had moved to 829 Eleventh Street.

During times of combat, a bugler was moved to the front line and acted as a stretcher carrier, taking the wounded off the battlefield and transporting them to a field hospital. While in the line of this duty on October 21, 1918, at Hill 255 in the Argonne Forest, Bugler Curry was hit by a bullet and died.

Upon learning of his heroic death, his mother opted to have Charles buried in a military cemetery. He was laid to rest at Fort Rosecrans National Cemetery in San Diego in Section Ps-8, Site 449.

FRANK EUGENE SPERRY

Private – Company B, 363th Infantry, 91ˢᵗ Division

Frank was born on New Year's Day in 1895 in Vernalis, Stanislaus County, to Eugene and Bernice Sperry. He was one of 10 children born to the couple. He lived most of his life in Modesto and Vernalis. In the 1917 draft, Frank was living in Vernalis and working in Tracy as a mechanic for Josh Brown. This is most likely why his name was included in the list of soldiers from San Joaquin County.

Frank was part of the second contingency from Stanislaus County, leaving for Camp Lewis on October 6, 1917. He was assigned as a mechanic in Company B, 364ᵗʰ Infantry of the 91ˢᵗ Division. This unit participated in the Fall Offensive, making its way through the Argonne Forest.

Private Sperry was shot in the hip and side on September 1918. He was taken to a field hospital but never recovered from his wounds. He died on October 14, 1918. He was buried in the American Expeditionary Forces military cemetery near the hospital in France.

His family chose to have his body sent home to Modesto in 1921. He was buried in the IOOF Section of Modesto's Pioneer Cemetery.

HERBERT HOVARD

Private – Company E, 59ᵗʰ Infantry, 89ᵗʰ Division

Herbert was born in Culbertson, Nebraska, on July 6, 1890, to Noah and Olive "Ollie" (McAdow) Hovard. The family had moved to Richland, Nebraska, by the 1900 Census. In the 1910 Census, they were living on a farm on Alpine Road south of Kettleman Lane in rural Lodi. When Herbert registered to vote in 1912, he stated he was a farmer.

When he completed his draft registration in June 1917, Herbert was working as an electrician for the California Hydraulic Engineering and Supply Company out of San Francisco. He still lived in Lodi.

Herbert was sent to training at Camp Funston, Kansas. He was attached to Company E of the 59ᵗʰ Infantry, 89ᵗʰ Division. They were transported to France on May 5, 1918, aboard the ship *Olympic*.

The 89ᵗʰ Division fought in many significant battles during the St.

Mihiel and Meuse-Argonne campaigns under the command of Major General Leonard Wood. Private Hovard was declared missing in action in the Meuse-Argonne on October 14, 1918. His body was later found, and he was buried in France. His date of death is listed as the same day he went missing.

His family requested that his body be sent back to Lodi. It was returned on the army transport ship *Wheaton* on August 6, 1921. His final resting place is in Lodi Memorial Cemetery.

THOMAS WILBER HUGILL

Corporal – Company L, 363ʳᵈ Infantry, 91ˢᵗ Division

Thomas was born in Stockton on February 26, 1893. His parents were Jonathan and Mary Rebecca (Powell) Hugill. He was their only son. His father, who was born in Canada, died in 1897 and was buried in the Woodbridge Cemetery. His mother moved in with her brother in the Elkhorn Township north of Stockton, and Thomas worked on the farm.

Thomas was in the second contingency from Stockton, leaving by train for Camp Lewis on September 19, 1917. While at camp, Hugill earned the rank of Corporal and was attached to Company L of the 363ʳᵈ Infantry, 91ˢᵗ Division. In this company were other young men from San Joaquin County. Because of his high marks at Camp Lewis, Thomas was one of the 1,000 young men given a tour through Canada on their way to Camp Merritt, New Jersey.

The unit departed for France on July 7, 1918, on the ship *Benalla*. It had spent over six months training. Upon arrival, the 91ˢᵗ Division was put to the test. The men were with General John J. Pershing as he fought at the front line during the Meuse-Argonne Offensive, which began on September 26. Corporal Hugill survived the fighting in France, and was soon sent to Belgium.

Corporal Hugill was killed in action on October 31, 1918, while fighting in Belgium on the first day of the battle at Ypres-Lys. He was buried where he fell. Later, he was interred in the Flanders Field American Cemetery in Waregem, Belgium. He rests in Plot C, Row 2 - Grave 22. Sergeant Karl Ross of Stockton was killed on the same day in the same battle. He, too, is buried in Flanders Field.

PHILIP (FELIPE) B. MONTOYA

Private – Company L, 354th Infantry, 89th Division

Philip was born on August 23, 1892, to Santiago and Elefanito Montoya in Las Vegas, New Mexico. His father died before 1900, leaving his mother to raise three young sons. Each of them had to find work at an early age. In 1910, Philip was working as a printer in Las Vegas.

At the time of the 1917 draft, Philip was working as a farm laborer for Tony Soares on Roberts Island just west of Stockton. It is unknown why he left New Mexico for work in Stockton. He enlisted while in San Joaquin County but was sent to Camp Funston, Kansas, to join others from his home state.

While at camp, Philip was assigned to Company L of the 354th Infantry, 89th Division. They were transported on June 5, 1918, to France aboard the ship the *Ascanius* from Montreal, Canada. The Middle West Division (the 89th) was comprised of young men from Kansas, Missouri, Arizona, New Mexico, Colorado, Nebraska and South Dakota.

The 89th fought in the Battle of Saint Mihiel from September 12 – 15, 1918. This was the first battle with the American Expeditionary Forces taking the lead. They were under the command of General John J. Pershing. The AEF committed 550,000 men, 419 tanks, 1,481 aircraft and 2,900 artillery to engage in this fight. Slogging through five days of steady rain with full tank support, the Americans surprised the Germans and sent them into retreat. This established their stature in the Allies' eyes.

But the muddy terrain caused supplies to be left along the way, with 4,500 men killed and another 2,500 wounded. Philip survived this battle, and soon afterward, the 89th was sent to the Argonne Forest. Pershing believed the time was right to force the Germans into further retreat. The Battle of Meuse-Argonne began on September 26 and carried on for 45 days.

On October 31, 1918, Private Montoya was killed in action. His body was temporarily buried near where he fell. Later, he was buried in the Meuse-Argonne American Cemetery. But his family requested he be brought back to New Mexico. Philip's final resting place is in the Santa Fe National Cemetery, Plot A-1, Grave 1187.

KARL ERSKINE ROSS

Sergeant - Machine Gun Company, 363rd Infantry, 91st Division

Karl was born June 27, 1894, in Petaluma, California. His father, David Ross, was born in Scotland and in 1900 was employed as the superintendent of a copper mine in Amador County. Karl's mother, Caroline Lucy Jones, died on March 11, 1903, and is buried in the Sutter Creek Cemetery. His father married Carrie May Wilbur in 1905, and the family moved to Stockton by the 1910 Census. David had family members who owned the Ross Mercantile Agency in Stockton.

In 1910, Karl was 16 and worked as a carrier for *The Stockton Record*. His father, David, was still working at the copper mine, Karl's brother Arthur was an advertising solicitor for the paper, and his other brother, Alan, was a collector for the Mercantile Agency. In 1912, Karl joined Alan as a collector for the agency. The family resided at 545 Poplar Street. By 1914, Karl was working as a clerk for the American Gasoline Company, and when he completed his draft card in 1917, he was a clerk for Shell Oil.

Karl was drafted and sent to Camp Lewis in Washington. He was one of the first 5% of Stockton's quota expected to serve. He was assigned to the 91st Division, 363rd Machine Gun Company. The 363rd shipped out of Hoboken, New Jersey, on July 7, 1918. The 363rd included other area young men such as Frank Elsholz, Eugene Fitzsimmons, John Steele, Jess Linley (all of Stockton), Earl Woodward of Lathrop and Fritz Tugel of Manteca. The 363rd, along with the Machine Gun Company, included Companies I, K, L, and M. Many other local young men were attached to these units and were aboard the *Benalla*.

Karl Ross was an admirable soldier. While fighting in the European campaign, he was promoted to the rank of Sergeant just days before his death.

His division fought in the Meuse-Argonne Offensive at the end of September, where he was slightly wounded. His actions on October 31, 1918, at Ypres-Lys/Waregem in West Flanders, Belgium, which resulted in his death, created the opportunity for his captain to recommend him for the Distinguished Service Cross.

"At a distance of less than 200 meters from the enemy, Sgt Ross set up and directed the fire of his guns, exposed during the whole operation to direct enemy fire. He killed one gunner and, while searching for the Hun on his flank, was killed himself."

He was awarded the honor posthumously, and the Cross is on display in the atrium of Karl E. Ross American Legion Post 16.

Karl's body originally was buried by the chaplain of his division directly on the field where his body lay. He eventually was moved to Flanders Field American Cemetery in Waregem, Belgium, where he now rests in Plot B, Row 1 - Grave 3. His father died two months later and was buried in Park View Cemetery, Manteca.

NB: The quotation was taken from the actual account submitted by his superior officer for consideration of an official citation. The American Government determined he met the criteria of "exceptional heroism and conspicuous service above and beyond the call of duty."

SAVIO JOSEPH FUGAZZI

Private – Company L, 363ʳᵈ Infantry, 91ˢᵗ Division

Savio was born in Stockton to Giuseppe and Carollatta Fugazzi on February 5, 1892. The family resided in the Garden Colony of northeast Stockton and had lived there for more than 40 years. This area was populated by many Italian Immigrants, some of whom had helped form the Italian Gardener's Society in 1902. On his 1917 draft registration, Savio stated he was farming with his father.

Savio enlisted soon after the draft in September 1917 and was sent along with many other local young men to Camp Lewis, Washington. While in basic training, he was assigned to Company L of the 363ʳᵈ Infantry, 91ˢᵗ Division. On July 7, 1918, the company shipped out from Hoboken, New Jersey, on the *Benalla* headed for France.

Private Fugazzi was involved in the Meuse-Argonne Offensive and was part of the division that fought for 10 straight days as they went "over the top." The 91ˢᵗ was then placed in the rear for a 10-day rest. But the 363ʳᵈ Infantry was ordered to go back into battle immediately, temporarily attached to the 1ˢᵗ Division. They finally were given a three-day rest.

Savio survived the battle of Meuse-Argonne. But at the end of October, the entire 91ˢᵗ division was sent to join the French troops in Waregem, Belgium, and fought valiantly in the Ypres-Lys campaign near Flanders Field. Private Fugazzi was wounded on the first day, October 31, 1918, and he succumbed to his wounds two days later. He was buried near the field hospital.

On May 18, 1921, Savio's body arrived back in Stockton. His final interment was in the Stockton Rural Cemetery. Karl Ross American

Legion Post 16 provided the honor guard and bugler at the funeral service. It was quite fitting, since Sergeant Ross was one of Savio's comrades-in-arms who had fallen during the same battle on the same day.

CLINTON MCCAUSLAND

Sergeant – Company L, 363rd Infantry, 91st Division

Clinton was born in Linden, California, to James Audley and Caltha (Duff) McCausland on April 4, 1890. The family owned a farm in Dent, outside of Ripon. They had eight children; three sons and five daughters.

In the 1917 draft registration, Clinton stated that he was a self-employed farmer. He was sent to Camp Lewis in September 1917 with one of the early contingencies from San Joaquin County.

While at Camp Lewis, Clinton earned the rank of Private First Class and was attached to Company M of the 363rd Infantry, 91st Division. His unit was transported to France aboard the ship *Benalla* on July 7, 1918.

Sometime during his time in Europe, Clinton was reassigned to Company L of the 363rd, and he was promoted to Sergeant. His company fought in the Meuse-Argonne Offensive in the Belgium sector. He was killed in action on November 2, 1918.

The McCausland family had four of its children serve in the war. Audley, Clinton and Irvin were in the United States Army, while Agnes was a nurse for the American Red Cross. Audley temporarily left his position as the Ripon Postmaster, while Irvin joined the Army Medical Department in early 1917. Agnes would eventually become a nurse in the Naval Corps and would follow Audley as Postmistress in Ripon. To honor Clinton and his family, the newly formed American Legion Post 190 in Ripon was named the Clinton McCausland Post.

Sergeant McCausland's body was returned to Stockton on April 21, 1921, and he was buried with full honors in Park View Cemetery in Manteca. Karl Ross Post 16 conducted the ritualistic ceremony, and the Ripon American Legion provided the pallbearers, singers and bugler.

JACK AYK

Private – Company "I", 361st Infantry, 91st Division

Jack was born on February 9, 1893, in Amsterdam, Holland. His mother was Francina and his father is unknown. Jack spent seven years in the Dutch Navy. On October 5, 1916, he arrived in San Francisco from Java in the East Indies. He left his ship and went to find work.

In July 1917, when he completed his draft registration, he said he worked for Spreckels Sugar in Manteca and lived in Stockton. The Exemption Board member who interviewed him wrote, "In country 4 months and already speaks English." (Actually, he had been in California for eight months.) He obviously made an impression.

Jack was drafted and sent to Camp Lewis for training. He was assigned to Company "I" of the 361st Infantry, 91st Division. His company was transported on July 6, 1918, on the ship *Scotian*. He listed his mother, still living in Amsterdam, as his next of kin.

Private Ayk fought valiantly for three months with his company. He survived the battle of Meuse-Argonne from September 26 until October

5. After a 10-day rest, the 91st was reassigned to fight with the French Army in Belgium. The battle of Ypres-Lys near Flanders began on October 31. Jack was killed in action on November 4, 1918, just one week before the Armistice.

His final resting place is in the Flanders American Cemetery in Waregem, Belgium - Plot B, Row 4 - Grave 18.

DEWEY DAY SIVLEY

Private – 359th Infantry, 90th Division

Dewey Day was born July 1899 in Arkansas and was named for the famous admiral of the Spanish-American War. At a young age, he traveled to Stockton with his older brother George, who was the manager of Woolworth's Department Store. Dewey was employed at the Hotel Clark; but when he turned 18, he traveled to the state of Washington to enlist.

He was originally assigned to an aviation unit but was eventually transferred to the 359th Infantry, 90th Division. Private Sivley was killed in action while fighting in the Meuse-Argonne on November 5, 1918, at only 19 years of age. His father, George W., had died just weeks prior on October 5, 1918. His brother and sister asked that Dewey's body be sent back to Stockton. He was buried in Stockton Rural Cemetery alongside his father.

LARS PETER LARSEN

Private – 9th Infantry, 2nd Division

Lars Peter Larsen was born June 24, 1891, in Denmark. Not much is known about his early life. He may have immigrated to the United States in 1911 as there is a ship's manifest that matches his age.

In 1917 when he completed the draft registration, he was working on a farm owned by E. Fanter on French Camp Road. He lived at 26 S. El Dorado Street in Stockton.

Lars was drafted and sent to Camp Lewis for training. His name was redrawn in the replacement draft (a draft to fill regiments that were on their way to France). So, without much time in camp, he departed on March 16, 1918, for France. He stated his next of kin was his cousin Lois Jessen, who lived in Benson, Nebraska.

Upon arrival in France, Private Larsen was assigned to the 2nd Division's 9th Infantry. He fought with his company for months and participated in the final days of the Meuse-Argonne Offensive. He was killed in action on November 6, 1918, and is buried in the Meuse-Argonne American Cemetery in Romagne, France. He rests in Plot A, Row 42 - Grave 30.

JOSEPH FRED SMITH

Private – 12th Battery, 8th Division

Joseph was born at Clay Station in rural Sacramento County on February 2, 1893, to Charles and Delilah Smith. The Smiths owned a farm on Clay Station Road, where Joseph spent most of his young life. He attended Galt schools and in 1917 went to work for Southern Pacific

Railroad. His area was in the northeast corner of San Joaquin County and the adjoining southeast corner of Sacramento County. Sometime in late 1918, he left Southern Pacific and took a job at the Utah Condensed Milk Company in Galt, which enabled him to stay closer to home.

In fall of 1918, Joseph entered the Army. He was sent to Camp Fremont and assigned to the 12th Battery of the 8th Division. After just two months in camp, the division received orders to be transported to Siberia.

Russia was undergoing civil conflict. The United States Government had been sending great amounts of ammunition, food and other supplies to Eastern Russia in support of Russia's efforts in the European theater. Now these supplies were being threatened by Cossack marauders and Japanese military. President Wilson ordered the 8th division to Siberia with the purpose of protecting those supplies. Additionally, the Czech army was being detained in Siberia as it attempted to reach the Western Front. Wilson wanted our troops to assist with their evacuation and provide military personnel to operate the Trans-Siberian Railroad.

The 8th Division began sending 5,000 men to the desolate frozen terrain of Eastern Russia. They were assigned to Vladivostok and Arkhangelsk (Archangel). Joseph was sent from Camp Fremont to Fort Mason in San Francisco. He was transported aboard the ship *Logan* on September 2, 1918, heading for Honolulu. From there, the troops would sail to Russia.

Unfortunately, the area was not safe, and the men were miserable. The temperature made it impossible to perform simple tasks. The horses used for wagon transport struggled to survive in the harsh climate. Machine guns froze. Fuel did not function properly. The United States Army was not prepared for such a challenge.

There was much civil unrest in the area, and soldiers faced constant fear of skirmishes with the locals. On February 10, 1919, Joseph was killed during one of the multiple insurrections. His parents were not given much detail of his death. His body was shipped home, and he was buried in the Galt Cemetery alongside his father. His sister lived in Lodi, which may explain why his name is on the plaque of soldiers from San Joaquin County.

WALTER WILLIAM FIGGINS

Private – Company D, 116th Engineers, 41st Division

Walter was born May 7, 1896, in Fresno, California, to Isabelle and Alvin Figgins. When he was 4 years, old his parents divorced, and his mother moved with her eight children to Merced. But by 1916, the Figgins family was living at 231 S. East Street in Stockton. Walter got a job as an engineer for Holt Tractor while his brother William worked there as a machinist.

The Holt Tractor Company had signed a contract with the Allies to provide hundreds of Holt tread- system tractors for towing heavy cannon and moving other materials across the boggy ground of Belgium and France. The company was hiring able workers.

By the 1917 draft, Walter was working on a farm owned by Albert Lindley on Rough and Ready Island. He was one of Stockton's early recruits, and he was assigned to the 41st Division, 116th Engineers - Company D, earning the rank of Private. His unit shipped out of Hoboken, New Jersey, November 26, 1917, on the *Tenadores*. His mother had married George Washington Burns, and they still resided on East Street.

Although his death is included in the list of Californians in the archive "American Soldiers of World War I," no date of death or burial information is included. His mother and stepfather eventually moved to Santa Rosa, while his father remained in Stockton.

MISSING IN ACTION

Fred Livermore	23 May 1918	at sea (*HMS Moldavia*)
Alexander Linde	25 Aug 1918	Somme (2nd battle)
Oliver James Stedman	29 Sep 1918	Meuse-Argonne (France)

FRED LIVERMORE

Private – 58th Infantry, 4th Division

Fred was born on August 19, 1888, to Henry and Concepcion (Rivera) Livermore in Livingston, California. In 1900, Henry was the postmaster of the small town of Panoche in Fresno County. He and his wife had 10 children. Henry died in 1902, leaving Concepcion a young widow.

In 1912, Fred lived in Stockton at 813 E. Main and was working as a painter. He lived at various addresses (214 S. Grant, 603 E. Lindsay and 129 Bridge Street) but always was listed as a painter in the City of Stockton Directory.

When Fred completed his draft registration in 1917, he was living at the Hotel Mason. He joined the Army and became a private in the 58th Infantry of the 4th Division – The Ivy Division.

Private Livermore was being transported to England with 53 other soldiers from his company aboard the HMS *Moldavia*. On May 23, 1918, the *Moldavia* was hit by a torpedo launched from a German U-boat. The ship sunk off Beachy Head in the English Channel. All 54 from the 58th Infantry went down with the ship. Their bodies were not recovered.

The names of the soldiers from the 58th are etched on the Tablets of the Missing at Brookwood American Cemetery in Surrey, England. They are among a total of 563 names on the tablets, mostly men from the US Navy and US Coast Guard who lost their lives on the sea.

Today, the *Moldavia* has been designated as a War Memorial under the Protection of Military Remains Act of 1986. The wreck site is protected and may be dived, but nothing can be removed, and no one can enter the vessel. She is now considered a war grave. Private Fred Livermore is laid to rest in this watery grave.

ALEXANDER LINDE

Private – Company I, 47ᵗʰ Infantry, 4ᵗʰ Division

Alexander was born in Heilbrum, Russia, to John and Helena Linde on September 19, 1891. He was one of 10 children. The Lindes were of German descent, having settled in Russia by invitation of the Russian Government. But by 1900, the family had immigrated to Mercer, North Dakota, most likely with many others from their Russian community. The Linde family remained in Mercer until sometime after 1910.

In the 1917 draft registration, Alexander noted that he was a naturalized United States citizen and worked as a machinist for the George West & Son Winery in Victor, California. He lived with his family on Harney Lane, about 5 miles southeast of Lodi. Prior to him leaving for the military, Alexander was promoted to head winemaker and was well-known in the Lodi wine world.

Alexander left for Camp Lewis with one of the first contingents from Lodi in September 1917. He spent five months training at Camp Lewis and then was assigned to a further month of training at Camp Greene in North Carolina, most likely as a replacement draftee. It was at Camp Greene that he was attached to Company I of the 47ᵗʰ Infantry, in the 4ᵗʰ Division. Their unit shipped out on May 10, 1918, aboard the ship *Caserta*.

Private Linde was engaged in battle for two months along the Western Front before he was killed in action by a shell explosion in No Man's Land on Flanders Field, Belgium, on August 25, 1918. His body was never recovered. His name is written on the Tablets of the Missing at the Oise-Aisne American Cemetery in Fere-en-Tardenois, France.

OLIVER JAMES STEDMAN

Private First Class – Company C, 363ʳᵈ Infantry, 91ˢᵗ Division

Oliver was born to James and Mary Stedman in Hollister, California, on December 20, 1893. The family still resided there in the 1900 Census; but by 1910, they had moved to the Manteca/Modesto area.

In the 1917 draft registration, Oliver wrote that he lived in Lathrop and was a farmer for A.S. Bromberg. Oliver left for Camp Lewis with one of the early San Joaquin contingencies in September 1917. He was attached to the 91st Division, 363rd Infantry in Company C. Their unit arrived in France in July 1918.

The 363rd was on the front line in late September 1918, fighting in the Argonne Forest. Oliver's company was heavily shelled and exposed to gas. Some of the injured men lay on the cold field for two days before being rescued.

Oliver's body was never recovered. He is officially listed as missing in action. His name is etched on one of the Tablets of the Missing at the Meuse-Argonne American Cemetery in Romagne, Lorraine, France. Posthumously, his parents received two Certificates of Commendation from Oliver's superior officers, relaying the bravery of their young son.

PRISONER OF WAR

Olien Rhodes	11 Nov 1918	Trier, Germany
George Lacey McCall	13 Feb 1919	Trier, Germany
Rollin Gentry Freshour	24 Aug 1919	Germany – but died in Ripon

OLIEN OSCAR RHODES

Private – Company G, 362nd Infantry, 91st Division

Olien was born to Eustace Howard and Lulu Martha Rhodes in Stockton on October 19, 1895. The family lived at 1612 E. Market Street. In the 1910 Census, Olien worked as a clerk in a clothing store. At the time of the 1917 draft registration, he was employed as a mill man for Harris Manufacturing. But at the time of his deployment, he was employed at Holt Manufacturing. He was part of the early contingencies from Stockton to take the train to Camp Lewis, Washington. Olien was attached to the 362nd Infantry of the 91st Division, Company G.

Sometime during the battle of Argonne, Olien was captured by the Germans. He had a broken leg and was sent to the German Prison Hospital in Trier, Germany. He was taken along with Private H.S. Killenborn. Private Rhodes never recovered from his injury, and he died on November 11, 1918. Private Killenborn wrote to the Rhodes family telling of Olien's death. Olien had given him his watch, pocketbook, some francs and a 5 German mark. So, Killenborn sent the family $30 along with the watch and pocketbook. He told of Rhodes' burial in the Trier Cemetery on November 14, 1918, with prayers said by a Lutheran priest.

In 1920, Private Rhodes was returned to the United States. He was buried in Arlington National Cemetery and lies at rest in Section 18 Site 1052.

GEORGE LACEY MCCALL

Sergeant – Company E, 348th Field Artillery, 91st Division

George was born May 8, 1893, in Stockton to David and Mary L McCall. By the 1910 Census, the family had moved to Ione. In 1917, George was hired by the JR Bradley Company as a farm implement salesman. He was assigned to the Reno area and moved to Ralston, Washoe County, Nevada. It was there that George completed his draft registration.

George was assigned to the 348th Field Artillery of the 91st Division and earned the rank of Sergeant. He served in Company E. Sometime during the 100-Day Offensive, Sergeant McCall was captured by the Germans and sent to their POW Camp in Trier, Germany. He died a prisoner on February 13, 1919, and was buried in the Trier Cemetery.

Eventually, Sergeant McCall's body was returned to the United States. He was interred in the San Francisco National Cemetery on October 1, 1920. His final resting place is at site 1246-A.

ROLLIN GENTRY FRESHOUR

Private – Company E, 116th Engineers, 41st Division

Private First Class – 24th Balloon Company, US Air Service

Rollin was born to William Andrew and Julia E. (Wright) Freshour in Jenny Lind, Calaveras County on February 4, 1896. He was one of four children. In the 1900 Census, the family was still in Jenny Lind; but in the 1910 Census, William had bought a dairy in Dent just outside of Ripon, California. Rollin worked on the dairy with his father, and in the 1917 draft, he stated that he also worked as a butcher at the Modesto Creamery.

Rollin left for France on the ship *Tenadores* on November 26, 1917. He was a private in Company E of the 116th Engineers, 41st Division. Sometime during his tenure in France, he was promoted to Private First Class and transferred to the 24th Balloon Company, United States Aero Service.

In June 1918, PFC Freshour was hit with shrapnel in the neck and leg. He lay for three days in the field before he was discovered by German soldiers. He was taken prisoner on June 6, 1918, and was put under the care of an older soldier.

According to POW records, Rollin was now a Sergeant in Company C of the 2nd Engineers. The Germans first sent him to Gemersheim, where he stayed for two weeks before being transported to a hospital in Rastadt. He said he was treated well and had access to food from the Red Cross; but his body was weak, and he struggled to recover. His weight dropped to 90 pounds.

He was a prisoner of war for six months and was moved two more times: first to Darmstadt and finally to Hamburg. Sometime in early December, he was released. He was assigned to a Military Police unit while trying to recover enough to be transported home. He finally was put on the ship *Pocahantas* on August 1, 1919, eight months after his release. He arrived by train in Ripon on August 16, but he was in very poor condition. He remained under his mother's constant care but succumbed to pneumonia on August 24, 1919.

DIED FROM WOUNDS

(Author's note: I have chosen to include only those soldiers who died of their wounds *after* Armistice. Those who died of wounds incurred during battle prior to November 11, 1918 are included with those killed in action. The exception is Private Wittmeier.)

Henry Wittmeier	9 Oct 1918	Gas Exposure/Lobar Pneumonia
Gasparo Cabutto	22 Nov 1918	Phosphene Gas Exposure
Roy Vernon Setzer	27 Jan 1919	Surgeries/Infection
Ernest Miller Bates	25 Jul 1919	Surgeries at Walter Reed Hospital
Frank S. Costa	Jul 1919	Wounded in Action

HENRY WITTMEIER

Private – 47th Infantry, 4th Division

Henry was born in Lehr, North Dakota, to Simon and Christian Wittmeier. He was one of 10 children. In the 1910 Census, the family was living on Jack Tone Road in Lockeford, California. In the 1917 draft registration, Henry wrote he was a farmer working for himself.

Henry was attached to the 47th Infantry of the 4th Division, most likely as a draft replacement. Private Wittmeier, and another young private from Montana were sent on a spy mission in No Man's Land (the area between the German and US/French lines) on August 5, 1918. They were discovered by a German spotlight, and the young men quickly saw a gas bomb heading toward them. Henry did not react in enough time and took the brunt of the gas as it exploded. Neither was able to speak, but the lad from Montana managed to crawl back to their company. He tried to explain where Henry lay, but he could not be understood.

Private Wittmeier lay in the open field for more than two days. When he finally was found, he was taken to a hospital; but he never spoke again. The gas did severe damage to his lungs, and he slowly slipped away. He died on October 9, 1918, in a French hospital after suffering for two months. The official cause of death was listed as lobar pneumonia. His body was transported to Lodi, and he was buried in Lodi Memorial Cemetery. The young soldier from Montana survived and sent the Wittmeiers a moving letter of Henry's bravery.

GASPARO PIETRO CABUTTO

Private – Company L, 353ʳᵈ Infantry, 89ᵗʰ Division

Gasparo was born June 22, 1888, in Genoa, Italy. He emigrated with his father, Natale, and mother, Eugenia, on May 19, 1897, aboard the ship *Werre*. The family first lived in New York but later joined hundreds of Genovese who moved to San Joaquin County. At the time of Gasparo's draft registration, his parents were living at 665 S. California Street. But Gasparo had found a job with a survey crew for the EP & SW Railroad and was working in Arizona. Gasparo enlisted and was sent to Camp Funston in Kansas. He was assigned to Company L, 353th Infantry in the 89ᵗʰ Division, which was formed on September 5, 1917.

The 353ʳᵈ regiment became known as They're from Kansas. They trained more than eight months before heading out to New Jersey on May 26, 1918. They boarded the ship *Pyrrhus* on June 4 with 111 officers and 3,401 enlisted men.

Upon landing in France, the regiment was assigned to the Reynal Training Area, where they stayed until August 4. From then on, these young men were engaged in major fighting: the Lucey Sector 5 campaign, the battle at St. Mihiel, and Euvezin Sector. Finally, they were put in reserve from October 9-19. But their rest was not long as they were sent immediately to the Bantheville Woods in the Meuse-Argonne. From the 19ᵗʰ of October until Armistice, they continued their battle through the woods of the Argonne Forest. After November 11, they were assigned as an Occupation Unit from Nov 24, 1918, until May 6, 1919. They returned to the United States on May 14, 1919, with 105 officers and 2,533 enlisted men.

But Private Cabutto was not one of those returning. Sometime during the final battle, the regiment was attacked with phosphene gas. Gasparo suffered immensely and died in a field hospital on November 28, 1918 (just 17 days after the Germans had surrendered). Gasparo was buried with many of his comrades in the Oise-Aisne American Cemetery in Fere-en-Tardenois, France – Plot A, Row 33 - Grave 14. His parents in Stockton received the telegram notifying them of his death just two days before Christmas.

NOTE: Gasparo's name is often written as Gaspare. His name on his draft registration and signature ends with an "e," but most of his military records end with an "o." *The Stockton Record* article and photo has his name with an "o," which is what I have chosen.

ROY VERNON SELTZER

Private – Company H, 157th Infantry, 40th Division
Private – Company M, 305th Infantry

Roy was born on July 20, 1894, in Jamaro, Illinois, to Joseph and Emma (Daugherty) Seltzer. He had a twin sister named Floy Ferne. In 1900, the family lived in Perry County, Illinois; but soon after, Joseph and Emma divorced. Emma moved to Lodi, California, taking the twins and her daughter Lillian. Joseph moved to Alameda County, taking his two older boys with him.

In the 1917 draft, Roy stated he lived at 227 N. Sacramento Street in Lodi and worked as a waiter for the Shamrock Grill. He was sent to Camp Lewis in April 1918 and was transferred to Camp Kearny in San Diego in July. Private Seltzer was attached to Company H, 157th Infantry of the 40th Division, most likely as a replacement draftee.

The 157th was transported to France on August 8, 1918, on the ship *Osterley*. He was transferred to Company M, 305th Infantry. In late September, Private Seltzer's unit was engaged in the battle of the Argonne Forest. On October 5, after fighting for several days, Roy was hit twice in the left leg with bullets from a machine gun.

On October 8, it was determined that his leg needed surgery. He was sent to the base hospital, where he developed a post-operative infection that resulted in pulmonary difficulties. Because of these complications, he remained in the hospital for several months. In the meantime, armistice was declared in November.

Finally deemed fit to travel back to the States, Private Seltzer was placed on the transport *Mongolia* on January 19, 1919. He did not make it home alive. While in transport, weak from his wounds, the surgery, and his compromised lungs, he died of pneumonia on January 27, 1919. His body was sent back to Lodi, and he was buried next to his mother in Lodi Memorial Cemetery, Pioneer II, Block 3, Lot 6.

ERNEST MILLER BATES

Private – Company M, 361st Infantry, 91st Division

Ernest was born on the Fourth of July, 1894, in Fort Worth, Texas. His parents were Thomas Fuller Bates and Hettie (Rouff) Bates. In 1917, just in time for the draft registration, Ernest took a job in Stockton with Castle Printing Company as a pressman. He boarded with the S.H. Owen family at 105 E. Flora. The Owens were leaders of the local YMCA.

Ernest joined the First Christian Church and was a member of its choir. He was an amiable lad, well-liked by all who met him. In 1918, he left Castle Printing to work at Atwood Printing. He enlisted in the Army and left for Camp Lewis on June 20, 1918.

In a record three days, Ernest was assigned to Company M of the 361st Regiment and left for France immediately. The regiment arrived in just 26 days, the shortest amount of time for any West Coast unit.

While in France, the 361st participated in most of the significant battles. It was assigned to the front line during the 100-Days Offensive in the Argonne Forest. Private Bates was shot in the left hip on October 9, 1918. But due to heavy fighting, he could not be rescued. He lay on the battlefield for two days before the ambulance crew could retrieve him.

He was immediately sent to a dressing station, then to a local hospital in France. He remained in the hospital for six months before doctors felt it was safe for him to travel. He was sent back to the United States and brought to the Walter Reed Reconstruction Hospital in Washington,

D.C.. There he underwent 10 painful operations.

On July 25, 1919, Private Bates finally succumbed to his wounds and to the extensive trauma his body had endured. His mother had moved to Shreveport, Louisiana, so his body was sent to her. He was buried in Greenwood Cemetery.

FRANK S. COSTA

Private – Battery A, 146th Field Artillery

According to his 1917 draft registration card, Frank was born on December 20, 1896, in Marshall, Sonoma County, California. At the time, he was a farmhand for A. J. Morris, living in Holt just west of Stockton. When he enlisted in the Army, he was assigned to the 146th Field Artillery, Battery A. He was transported with his unit on December 24, 1917, on the White Star liner *Lapland*. He listed his cousin Emil Costello of San Rafael as his next of kin.

He was wounded sometime during battle (date and place unknown). Private Costa died in 1919 from his wounds, according to military records. His place of burial is not known.

ACCIDENTS

William Valjean Schleiger	15 May 1918	train wreck
Loui Charles Beauman	23 Mar 1918	seaplane fall
James Edward King	Oct 1918	own gun misfired
Harry L. Mercer	14 Nov 1918	USS Louisville explosion
George Mauch	29 Nov 1918	drowning
Charles Chilton Moore, Jr.	unknown	unknown

WILLIAM VALJEAN SCHLEIGER

Private– Company A, 116th Engineers, 41st Division
Private First Class - 11th Company, Transport Corps

William V. Schleiger was born in Sutton, Nebraska, on August 25, 1889. Not much is known about his early life, but he lived in Portland, Oregon, in the early part of the century. His sister remained there and always was listed as his next of kin. His parents were originally from Holland.

William worked for the Southern Pacific Railroad. In 1910, he was working in the rail shops in Portland and lived at 519 Commercial Street. His job brought him to Stockton, where he lived in 1917. On his draft registration, he stated he was a yardman at the Stockton Yard, but City of Stockton directories for 1916 and 1917 list him as a switchman.

In August 1917, William enlisted in the Army and was assigned to the 116th Engineers, a railroad unit. It departed on November 26, 1917, for France aboard the ship *HR Mallory*. This group of young men had the task of laying track and building rail lines to enable supplies to be delivered to the troops at the front. It was part of the logistics quickly organized by our Army Corps of Engineers.

While driving a locomotive near La Beaule, France, one of the cars derailed. It toppled the engine and killed Private Schleiger. He was buried nearby. On August 24, 1920, his body was returned to the United States on the transport ship *Princess Matoika*. The ship's manifest stated that he had been transferred to the 11th Company of the Transport Corps and promoted to Private First Class. His body was sent to his sister in Portland, where he was laid to rest in Lincoln Memorial Park, Veteran's Plot Section F.

LOUI CHARLES BEAUMAN

2nd Lieutenant – Aeronautic Detachment,
Naval Air Station; USMC

Loui was born in Hondo, Mexico, to Loui and Carrie Elizabeth "Kittie" Woodruff Beauman. His father was a Captain in the US Engineer Corps at the time of his birth. By the 1910 US Census, the family had moved to Los Angeles. In the 1912 Stockton City Directory, Mr. Beauman was now employed as a division engineer for the Southern Pacific Railroad, and the family resided at 1245 W. Magnolia Street.

Loui Charles graduated from Stockton High School in 1912 and enrolled at Stanford University. Within a year, he transferred to UC Berkeley, where he became a member of Zeta Psi Fraternity, was active in theater (once performing in *Twelfth Night*) and graduated with honors in 1917 with a degree in letters and science,

Upon graduation, Loui took a job in Salt Lake City, Utah; but he immediately enlisted in the US Navy on May 22, 1917, and was commissioned as an Ensign. He was sent back to California for training at Mare Island from June 18 to July 14, 1917.

Muster rolls show that, in July, L. C. received "undisclosed" orders to report to the Marine Barracks at Quantico, Virginia. He was transferred into the Marine Corps and given the rank of 2nd Lieutenant. He remained "under instruction" at Quantico from mid-July until October 21.

Lt. Beauman then reported to the Marine Barracks at the Navy Yard in New York City and was assigned to the 61st Company. In February 2018, he was detached to the Marine Barracks in Philadelphia and shortly thereafter was sent to an Aeronautic Detachment at the Naval Air Station in Miami, Florida.

While in Florida, Loui was in flight training, specifically learning to fly sea planes. He tragically fell from his plane during a training exercise and suffered a fractured skull. He died on March 23, 1918.

Notification of his death was received by the local Stockton Masonic Lodge, in which Loui had been bestowed the honor of Knights Templar. Lodge members said it was rumored that Loui had been training for a secret mission that was to take place in France.

2nd Lieutenant Loui C. Beauman was laid to rest at Arlington National Cemetery in Section 2, grave 2398 on the West Side. Soon after his death, Loui's father re-enlisted in the Army Corps of Engineers. He served as Captain of the 48th Engineers from July 1918 until his return to Berkeley and civilian life May 1919.

JAMES EDWARD KING

Carpenter's Mate 3rd Class – United States Navy

James was born in Texas around the year 1899. In 1915, he moved to Roberts Island, west of Stockton, with his sister Daisy and her husband, Zebulon Columbus Lytle. Zeb was working as a telegraph operator for the Santa Fe Railroad.

James enlisted in the Navy on June 29, 1917, in San Francisco, California. He was only 18 years old. He became a Carpenter's Mate and was sent in October 1917 to Pauillac, France, and assigned to the Naval Air Station. This station, which opened in December 1917, was home to the Navy's newly formed seaplane division.

Third Mate King died from accidentally discharging his weapon on November 2, 1918. His mother, Iona, had moved to Woodsboro in Los Angeles County. Daisy and her husband had moved to Muir Station near Martinez. The family chose to bring his body home to San Francisco, the place where he had enlisted. James King was buried in San Francisco at the National Cemetery in Plot N.

HARRY LEON MERCER

Fireman 2nd Class – United States Navy

Harry was born in Denver, Colorado, on April 7, 1893. He married Julia H. Doran in Denver on October 8, 1913, and the couple moved to Stockton, residing at 1031 N. Harrison. He got a job working as a clerk.

In the 1917 draft registration, they lived at 1022 S. San Joaquin Street and he was a builder for Holt Manufacturing. Harry stated he was married with a child (Mary Helen, born July 26, 1914) and had previously served in the Artillery.

In 1918, Harry enlisted in the Navy. He was assigned to the *USS Louisville* as a Fireman 2nd Class. On November 24, 1918, at 9:30 a.m., the following occurred: "In port engine room bonnet and body of cut-out valve on auxiliary steam line above boiler #2 carried away." Three men were killed, one officer and two enlisted men, including Harry Mercer.

He was buried at the Cypress Hills National Cemetery in Brooklyn, New York; Section 2, Site 7924. His wife and daughter moved to New York, and remained there the rest of their lives.

GEORGE MAUCH

3rd Class Cook – United States Navy

George was born on October 11, 1895, in New Salem, North Dakota, to John and Magdalene Mauch. The family moved to Lodi, and George got a job working on a local ranch. His sister Johanna moved to Stockton and found a job in the pencil factory.

In 1917, when George completed his draft registration, he was living in Salt Lake City employed as a cook in a restaurant. Due to his culinary knowledge, he joined the Navy as a Cook.

He was assigned to *USS Clapet* #4, which did transport duty through the Panama Canal. On November 29, 1918, the ship was docked and a ladder was placed onto the ground to use as a gangway. George slipped as he walked across the ladder, fell into the water and drowned.

Cook Mauch's body was sent back to his mother, who resided at 523 Hilborn Street in Lodi. He was laid to rest in Lodi Memorial Cemetery.

CHARLES CHILTON MOORE, JR.

Lieutenant –

Lieutenant Charles Chilton Moore, Jr. is found on the list of *American Soldiers of World War I*. His hometown was Middle River, San Joaquin County, California. This is an area on the western edge of the county heading towards Discovery Bay on Highway 4. His date of death is 1917-1918, under "accidents."

No records can be found on this soldier. One can assume that he was a college graduate since he was a lieutenant. There is a young man with the same name who was born in 1897 and attended Massachusetts Institute of Technology in 1917. No direct link can be made to a military record of the same name.

SPANISH INFLUENZA

According to information from the National Institutes of Health, the Spanish Influenza pandemic and World War 1 were closely entwined. The crowded conditions of a soldier's life was a petri dish for this illness. Camps overflowed with young men who were exhausted from their daily training, thus compromising their resistance to infection. Trenches were a bacterial nightmare – wet, dirty and often unsanitary. And the transporting on trains and ships in close quarters of men who were already sick with the disease only magnified the problem.

It was estimated that between 20 and 40% of the military became ill with either influenza or pneumonia. More resources were diverted to support the sick and dead than used for combat. It also is estimated that approximately one million men died before they ever got to France.

Exacerbating the issue were the climate conditions in training camps in the Pacific Northwest, especially Camp Lewis. The constant rain and damp bred colds and pneumonia. When the soldiers loaded on trains for transport across the United States, they already were contagious. As the trains picked up additional men along the way, the disease spread. Recent research now suspects that Ground Zero for our military was Camp Funston in Kansas. By the time the train got to Camp Merritt in New Jersey, many were sick and already dying. Camp Merritt's military hospital was full to the brim.

INFLUENZA AND OTHER DISEASES

Arthur J. Spencer	13 May 1917	pneumonia	Ft. McDonald CA
Oscar S. Mortensen	1 Jan 1918	illness	Ft. Sheridan IL
William C. Rossi	22 Jan 1918	tuberculosis	
Millard F. Brown	2 Feb 1918	appendicitis	Mare Island CA
Henry Herbert Gage	7 Feb 1918	measles	Del Rio TX
John D .Yount	15 Feb 1918	cancer	Spartanburg SC
Henry J. Trimberger	9 Jul 1918	heart attack	San Diego CA
Earl David Hickey	29 Jul 1918	meningitis	Coast of Ireland Aboard USS Destroyer *Allen*
Paul E. Carrier	22 Sep 1918	bronc-pneum.	New London CT
Harold Leroy Higgins	22 Sep 1918	influenza	Camp Merritt NJ
Karl I. Bradigan	26 Sep 1918	influenza	Newport RI

Cornelius Harrison	4 Oct 1908	influenza	Camp Sills WA
William Anthony Fisher	6 Oct 1918	pneumonia	Vancouver WA
Vernon Thomas Dragoo	12 Oct1918	pneumonia	
John E. Casenave	15 Oct 1918	bronc-pneum.	Ft Sam Houston TX
Charles R. Patten	15 Oct 1918	pneumonia	Ft Omaha NE
William Vernon White	15 Oct 1918	influenza	at sea
George Joseph Pahl	17 Oct 1918	pneumonia	Ft. Omaha NE
Leroy R. Foster	18 Oct 1918	pneumonia	France
Theodore Englar Royer	23 Oct 1918	influenza	Camp Johnson FL
Roy Lincoln Estes	24 Oct 1918	influenza	SF Presidio CA
Vivian Ashley Dodd	29 Oct 1918	pneumonia	Windsor NS Australia
Olaf E. Nelson	31 Oct 1918	influenza	Vancouver WA
Elmer Haub	Oct 1918	influenza	San Diego CA
Glenn W. Bush	9 Nov 1918	influenza	Camp Kearny CA
Romain Schell	9 Nov 1918	influenza	
Oscar Gulick	18 Nov 1918	influenza	Camp Upton NY
Thomas Shields DeHaven	19 Nov 1918	pneumonia	Kelly Field TX
Walter Lester Sievers	19 Nov 1918	pneumonia	Fort Crook NE
Virgil E. Pierce	27 Nov 1918	influenza	
Douglass Messersmith	Nov 1918	pneumonia	Siemscarey WA
Ora F. Winn	Dec 1918	influenza	Edmonton England
August Frey	6 Dec 1918	tuberculosis	at sea
John William Daly	25 Dec 1918	unknown	Stanislaus County CA
Richard Norton Coupe	1918	influenza	
William Brennan	1918	influenza	France
Bert Lewis	1918	influenza	France
Roy V. Seltzer	27 Jan 1919	pneumonia	at sea
Frederick D. Poindexter	30 Jan 1919	influenza	France
Walter Leslie Hunting	Jan 1919	influenza	Camp Hancock GA
Harry L. Rice	Feb 1919	bronch-pneum	France

Merrel Roy Battilana	29 May 1919	spinal meningitis	Goat Island (SF) CA
Sidney Brown	11 Jun 1919	cold	French Camp CA
William T. Littebrant	2 Jul 1919	pneumonia	Ft McClellan AL
Thomas Threlfall	14 Nov 1919	pulm hem.	Mil Hosp Aurora CO

ARTHUR J. SPENCER

Private – 17th Recruit Company, US Calvary

Arthur Spencer was the adopted son of Edwin Whitten Spencer and Lona Mina (Nichols) Spencer. According to the 1910 Census, Arthur was born in California sometime around 1899; but his burial information stated that he was born in 1898 in Clarksville, Butler County, Iowa. Edwin and Lona also had an adopted daughter, Vergie Viola, born in September 1898 in Nevada County, California. The Spencer family resided on Lockeford Street in Lodi. Edwin owned a vineyard, and he and Lona were photographers. Their studio was at 322 E. Pine Street.

Arthur originally joined the local militia in Stockton, a member of Battery C. He enlisted in the Cavalry at age 18 on February 13, 1917, and was sent to Fort McDonald in Marin County. Apparently, he was only there a short time when he came down with influenza. This developed into pneumonia, and he died on May 13, 1917. His body was sent back to Lodi, and he was buried in Lodi Memorial Cemetery, Section Pioneer II, Plot 26-1, next to Edwin, who had died in 1914.

OSCAR SOPHUS MORTENSEN

Private – 18th Regiment, 3rd US Army Corps of Engineers

Oscar was born on January 14, 1888, in Frederikshavn, Denmark. It is uncertain when he immigrated to the United States; but on his 1917 draft registration, he stated he was a "declarant with intent to become a naturalized citizen."

In August 1916, Oscar had been hired to work in the general shops of the Southern Pacific Railroad in Sacramento. His employment records show he was a machinist helper.

He quit his job with the railroad after only one week and began working for the Union Dredging Company on Venice Island as a leverman. He lived in the Carson Dredger Building on Bouldin Island. It appears that he may have enlisted and was assigned to the Army Corps of Engineers. This would be a natural transition since his 18th Regiment was building bridges and laying rail. He was sent to Fort Sheridan in Illinois for training.

Private Mortensen became ill in late December 1917. He died on January 1, 1918, and was buried in the Fort Sheridan Post Cemetery. He lies in Section 5, Site 434.

WILLIAM CHARLES ROSSI

Private –

William was born on October 31, 1895, in Fresno, California. On his 1917 draft registration card, he wrote that he was a self-employed farmer in the Elkhorn Precinct of Lodi. Information from the Army says that Rossi died of disease. No records have been found to provide any details, but he most likely died from influenza.

MILLARD FLETCHER BROWN

Electrician 3rd Class – United States Navy

Millard was born on March 26, 1898, in Leicester, Buncombe County, North Carolina. His parents were Filetus "Fleet" R. and Lou Ann Brown. The 1910 US Census has the family still living in Leicester; but by 1916, the family was on Church Street in Stockton. Millard was listed as a laborer.

Millard enlisted in the Navy and was assigned to the Naval Station at Mare Island. He was an Electrician 3rd Class. Unfortunately, his military career was cut short. He died on February 26, 1918, of acute appendicitis. His body was returned to Stockton, and he was buried in the Stockton Rural Cemetery Block 37.

HENRY HERBERT GAGE

Private – US Aviation Corps

Henry was born in Alva, Wyoming, to Herbert S and Emma Elizabeth Gage. He moved to California in 1910. In the 1917 City Directory, Henry was working on a farm in rural Escalon. He was too young for the draft, yet he enlisted in the Signal Corps in the newly created Aviation Department. He was sent to an aviation training center near Del Rio, Texas.

Soon after Private Gage arrived, he came down with the measles. He died on February 7, 1918, from appendicitis, which was identified on his death certificate as a complication of the measles. His body was sent to his parents in Alva, where he was buried in the local cemetery.

JOHN D. YOUNT

Corporal – Company D, 106th Infantry

John Yount was born in October 1880 in Shawnee, Kansas, to Frank and Laura (Thompson) Yount. In 1900, the family was living in Colorado Springs. On June 13, 1905, John married Louise Palmer in Houston, Texas. By 1910, they had moved to New York, and he enlisted in the New York National Guard, Company D in the 23rd Infantry of the 27th Division.

In the meantime, Frank and Laura had moved to Stockton. They owned a flower garden on Smith Tract. In the 1916 Stockton City Directory, John had a job with the Pacific Electric Railroad, where he was a substitute foreman.

John and Louise must not have stayed long in Stockton. He enlisted on June 12, 1917, in Brooklyn, New York. His National Guard unit was activated and transitioned to the 106th Infantry. It was sent to Camp Wadsworth in Spartanburg, South Carolina.

While in training, John fell ill. Doctors found a mediastinal tumor in the area between his heart and his lungs. He died on February 15, 1918, at the Spartanburg Base Hospital. His body was sent to Stockton, where he was buried in Stockton Rural Cemetery. His parents and his sister Katherine (Mrs. Homer Smith) remained in Stockton for the rest of their lives.

HENRY J. TRIMBERGER, JR.

Private – not assigned

Henry was born in December 1897 in California to Henry and Buletta Trimberger. The couple had emigrated from Denmark. In 1900, the family was living in San Francisco and Henry Sr. was a tallow maker. By 1910, they had a small farm in Elkhorn Township at the corner of Cherokee and Kettleman Lanes southeast of Lodi. Buletta had died, and Henry Jr. was helping his father on the farm.

Henry Jr. enlisted in 1918 and was sent to Camp Rosencrans in San Diego for basic training. On July 9, 1918, he suffered heart failure and died. He was only 20 years old. It is not known where he is buried. After his son's death, Henry Sr. sold his farm and moved with his daughter Gertrude to Oakland.

EARL DAVID HICKEY

Fireman 3rd Class – United States Navy

Earl was born in Walla Walla, Washington, in December 1899 to George and Grace Hickey. Sometime before 1910, the family moved to San Jose, where George was hired as a motorman for the San Jose Streetcar Company. Eventually, the family moved to Stockton and resided at 2459 E. Washington Street.

Earl worked for the department store Smith & Lang and played in the Holt Caterpillar Band. This band participated in the funeral cortege of many young soldiers being laid to rest in Stockton. When Earl turned 19, he went to Mare Island and enlisted on May 7, 1917.

Fireman Hickey was headquartered in Liverpool, England, and first assigned aboard the *Huntington*. Later he was sent to the destroyer *Allen*. While serving on the *Allen,* Earl became ill with influenza. He died on-board the ship as it sat off the coast of Ireland on July 29, 1918. Naval records showed the official cause of death was meningitis.

Earl's body arrived back in Stockton on September 27, and he was buried in Stockton Rural Cemetery. He was a member of the Woodmen of the World, who assisted with his funeral service.

PAUL EXCINA CARRIER

Quartermaster, 2nd Class – US Naval Reserve, New London CT

Paul was born in Los Angeles on December 18, 1896, to Paul E. and Katherine (Etcheverry) Carrier. His father was born in France, and his mother was from Spain. Paul was their firstborn, but the couple would go on to have five other children. Sadly, Mrs. Carrier died upon giving birth to their last child. At the time, the family resided in San Francisco.

By 1910, Mr. Carrier had moved with his young children to Stockton, where he worked as a chamois maker. Moving to Stockton allowed his children many opportunities. Paul Jr. attended business college and got a job as a stenographer for the Wagner Leather Company. He worked there four years but left to take a position as shipping clerk for the Sperry Flour Company.

Paul was considered one of the best athletes in Stockton. He pitched for the Sperry Athletics for three years and was known throughout the sporting circles in town. He was well-liked by those who met him.

On May 23, 1918, Paul enlisted in the Navy. In June, he was assigned to Mare Island and then transferred to San Pedro in southern California. At San Pedro, he was one of 25 young men selected from 500 applicants to be sent to Listener's School in Pelham Bay, New York. He was sent to New London, Connecticut, two weeks later and enrolled in a six-week listener's course.

He completed the course at the top of his class and was awarded the rank of 2nd Class Quartermaster. But in September, the New London Naval Base experienced an outbreak of influenza. Paul was admitted to the hospital on September 15 along with numerous other young men, and he died from bronchial pneumonia on September 22.

His father, still residing at 900 W. Washington Street, asked that Paul's body be sent back to Stockton. He was buried in Park View Cemetery in Manteca. Many Stocktonians attended his funeral in a display of gratitude and love.

HAROLD LEROY HIGGINS

Hospital Apprentice First Class – United States Naval Reserve

Harold was born July 1, 1894, in Sanborn County, South Dakota. His parents were Minnie Myrtle and Charles Higgins. The family moved to Oakland, where Charles got a job as a salesman for a construction supply company.

Harold registered to vote in Alameda County in 1916 and was in the Oakland City Directory in 1917. But sometime during that year, he moved to Stockton and got a job working for the newly built Owl Drugstore at 501 E. Main Street. This was the era when downtown businesses prided themselves in elaborate window displays. Harold was known by customers for the creative window decorations that wrapped around Main and American streets.

On June 27, 1918, Harold enlisted in the Naval Reserves at San Francisco. He became a Hospital Apprentice and was attached to the military hospital at Camp Merritt in New Jersey. This was a particularly dangerous job during the influenza outbreak that spread quickly throughout the camp.

Harold contracted the flu in late September and succumbed to the disease just two days later, on September 28. His body was sent back to his parents in Oakland, and he was buried in Mountain View Cemetery Plot 48 of that city.

KARL INGRAM BRADIGAN

Private – 98th Company, Naval Torpedo Training Center, USMC

Karl was born in Idaho in 1899. His mother died sometime before 1906, and his father moved to Alameda County, where he met and married Jennie Ingram in January of that year. By 1910, the family had moved to the town of Dent, a farming community east of Stockton.

In the 1917 City Directory, the family resided at 2566 E. Hazelton and young Karl was working at Sperry's Flour Mill as a packer.

Karl enlisted in the Marine Corps on September 25, 1917, just days after the first contingency of Stockton men left for Camp Lewis. He was only 19 years of age. He was assigned to Company E at Mare Island; and in November, he spent some time in the Naval Hospital. Upon release in December, he was transferred to the Marine Barracks at Quantico, Virginia.

From Quantico, Karl was transferred to the Marine Barracks at Newport, Rhode Island, where muster rolls show that he was in the 98th Company of the Naval Torpedo Training Center. He remained there from January 1918 until March, when he was sent to the Naval Ammunition Depot in New London, Connecticut, for additional training.

In May, Karl returned to the 98th Company in Newport. Unfortunately, he again spent many days in the hospital, first in the US Naval Hospital in Newport and then in the US Naval Hospital in Providence, Rhode Island. His military records also show that sometime in August upon release from the hospital, he went AWOL for two days. He was fined $20 and sentenced to 30 days of EP duty. Apparently, Karl's health continued to deteriorate. His obituary stated that he had surgery sometime prior to his death. Karl was readmitted back into the hospital in early September, and he died on the 26th of lobar pneumonia. His body was sent back to Stockton, and he was buried in Park View Cemetery, Manteca.

CORNELIUS HARRISON

Private – 91ˢᵗ Division, not assigned

Cornelius was born on August 18, 1897, in Bellota to John H. and Lily M. Harrison. The Harrison family owned a farm just east of Linden on Jenny Lind and Bellota roads. In the 1917 draft registration, Cornelius noted that he farmed with this father. His ethnicity was Ethiopian. He was drafted and sent to Camp Sims, the African-American barracks associated with Camp Lewis and the 91ˢᵗ Division.

Cornelius was not in camp long. He died, most likely of influenza, on October 4, 1918. His body was sent to Stockton by train, and he was buried on October 15 in Park View Cemetery in the Liberty Section. The City of Stockton honored his death like every other soldier: flags at half mast, the local band playing, and various organizations represented in the funeral cortege.

WILLIAM ANTHONY FISHER

Private – 15ᵗʰ Regiment, Spruce Division

William was the only child of Thomas E. Fisher and Minneta "Minnie" Earhart. He was born in Stockton on December 4, 1894. The family resided at 227 E. Sonora Street.

At the time of the draft, William was a carpenter, working for Charles A. Eldridge. But by 1918, he was employed by the Stockton Fire Department, serving at the Rose Street Station. His father was the assistant fire chief of the department.

William enlisted, was assigned to the 15ᵗʰ Regiment and was sent to the Vancouver Barracks in Washington for training. On October 4, 1918, his parents received a telegram that William was gravely ill with pneumonia. His mother left immediately for Vancouver, but she did not arrive in time. He died early Sunday morning, October 6.

His mother accompanied his body back to Stockton, and he was buried in the Stockton Rural Cemetery Block 17, E-26 with full honors from both the military and the Stockton Fire Department.

VERNON THOMAS DRAGOO

Private – 311th Supply Company, Quartermasters Corps

Vern was born January 25, 1895, in Gilroy, California, to John Arthur and Belle Zora Dragoo. In 1917, Vern was living in Porterville as a laborer. But in 1918, his parents moved to Stockton, living on S. California Street.

Vern was a Private in the Quartermasters Corps 311th Supply Company. His unit was part of the operational logistics moving food, ammunition and other supplies to the troops serving on the Western Front.

Sometime in early October 1918, Vern contacted Spanish Influenza. His body was weak, and on October 12, he died from bronchial pneumonia. His body was sent home to Stockton, and he was buried in the Stockton Rural Cemetery, Block 26.

JOHN E. CASENAVE

Private First Class – Troop E, 13th US Calvary

John grew up in Tuolumne County. He was born October 1895 to John Peter Casenave, who had emigrated from France, and his wife, Mary Veronica McFadden. John Peter made his living in the gold mines. Sometime after the 1910 US Census, the family moved to Stockton and resided at 548 N. California Street.

John enlisted in the Cavalry and was sent to Fort Sam Houston in San Antonio, Texas. He was assigned to Company E. While there, he contracted influenza. He died on October 15, 1918, from bronchial pneumonia. His body was returned to his parents in Stockton, and he was buried in the San Joaquin Catholic Cemetery.

CHARLES RUGGLES PATTEN

Lieutenant – 46th Balloon Company, Aviation Corps

Charles was born to Thomas Trueman and Flora (Martin) Patten on February 29, 1898, in Alexandria, Grafton, New Hampshire. Trueman was a carpenter by trade and moved the family to California in the early 1900's. They lived in San Mateo for awhile; but by 1915, he had secured a job with the Sperry Flour Mill in Stockton as its carpenter. They resided at 316 E. Walnut. Charles found a job as a clerk.

In the 1917 City Directory, Trueman and his sons moved to 1847 S. Sutter. Flora had died in 1916, and Charles now was working in his father's trade as a carpenter. He was a member of Carpenters Union Local 266 in Stockton.

On February 12, 1918, Charles enlisted in the Aviation Corps. He was sent to Kelly Field in Texas for basic training. While there, he showed good leadership skills and soon was promoted from Private to Lieutenant. (NOTE: This may be incorrect as it was highly unlikely for an enlisted man to be promoted to a rank usually given to a person with an educational background.)

While at Fort Omaha, Nebraska, the barracks experienced a terrible outbreak of Spanish Influenza. Charles became ill and developed pneumonia. He died on October 14, 1918. His father had his body sent to Lodi for burial in Lodi Memorial Cemetery, next to Flora. The funeral became Lodi's first military funeral.

WILLIAM VERNON WHITE

Cook – Ordinance Department

William was born in Woodbridge, California, on December 22, 1895, to Walter B. and Kate P. White. The Whites had two children: William and Olive, who became a teacher at Henderson School. William graduated from Lodi High School, and the family lived in the Kingdon District of Lodi.

William enlisted and joined the Agricultural and Mechanical Department of the Army. He was sent on June 13, 1918, to the State Agriculture College in Corvallis, Oregon, for special training in agriculture techniques. The Army's plan was to set up agricultural centers in Europe to begin producing fresh vegetables for the men on the line.

After William completed his two-month training, he was sent to Camp Hancock, Georgia awaiting further orders. At that time, the Army changed its philosophy regarding the agriculture experiment, so William decided to transfer to the Ordinance Department as a cook. Private White was sent to Camp Upton in New York and finally shipped overseas on October 10, 1918. Unfortunately, once on board, he became very ill with Spanish Influenza. He died five days out to sea.

His body was moved to a transport ship returning to the States and sent by train to Lodi. He was laid to rest in Lodi Memorial Cemetery Mausoleum. A tree was planted in his honor in the Woodbridge Cemetery with a plaque at its base.

GEORGE JOSEPH PAHL

US Signal Corps, Balloon Squadron, Aviation Section

George Pahl was born in Stockton on August 25, 1891, to Emil and Pauline (Dietrich) Pahl. Emil was the vice-president of Pahl & Harry Company, a Stockton plumbing company. George worked with his father and brothers and learned the sheet metal trade.

Sometime after the San Francisco earthquake, George and his brother August moved to Green Street in San Francisco. They worked together creating a plumbing and sheet metal company; finding much work as the city was in an extensive rebuild. George moved back to Stockton in 1912 and returned to the family business.

At the time of the draft registration in 1917, George was a master sheet metal worker. Perhaps this is why he was assigned to the Balloon Squadron of the Signal Corps and sent to Fort Omaha, Nebraska. In August 1917, the United States Aero Service restarted its observation balloon training program, which had been in its experimental stage in 1907. The project using dirigibles had been abandoned in 1909, but now the military saw a need and began rapid training at the Fort Omaha Balloon School.

But weather conditions were not suitable for training, so most of the companies were sent to Camp Wise in Texas in May 1918. Only a small ground group was left behind.

It appears that George was one of the crew left behind. In October 1918, Fort Omaha experienced an outbreak of Spanish Influenza. George contracted the disease, and he developed pneumonia. He died on October 17, 1918 (just two days after another local young soldier, Charles R. Patten, also died at Fort Omaha).

George's mother and sister, Clara, left Stockton and arrived in Nebraska to bring George's body back home. He is buried in Stockton Rural Cemetery, Block 24, Grave 57-D.

LEROY R. FOSTER

Private – 549th Motor Transport Corp

Leroy was born in January 1900 in Colton, Washington. His parents were Robert L. and Birdie (Rogers) Foster. The Fosters had five children: Leroy, the eldest, and four daughters. In the 1910 Census, the Fosters lived in San Jose, California, and Robert worked as a real estate agent. Later, the family moved to Ripon.

Leroy most likely enlisted. First, he was just 18, and second, he was exempt since he was an only son. Usually when a young man enlisted, he was assigned a non-battle position. This was probably true for Leroy. He was assigned as a driver in the Motor Transport Service. His job was to move soldiers and supplies in France, keeping in the background. Unfortunately, his job put him in contact with too many people. He contracted influenza and died of pneumonia on October 13, 1918.

Private Foster's body was buried in France and exhumed in 1920. He was shipped back to his parents in Ripon and laid to rest in the Modesto Pioneer Cemetery Block 19, Lot 4 - Grave 14.

THEODORE ENGLAR ROYER

Corporal – Quartermaster Corp

Theodore Royer was born in Waynesboro, Pennsylvania, to David and Effie G. (Shriner) Royer. The family moved to rural Fresno between 1910 and 1917. At the time of the draft, Theodore was working as a machinist for the San Joaquin Valley Farm Land Company. He was living in Fresno and stated he was a member of the Church of the Brethren. This church is considered one of the three historic peace churches, along with the Quakers and the Mennonites, and has a longstanding belief in pacifism and non-resistance.

Despite his religious beliefs, Theodore ended up in the Army. It is uncertain if he enlisted or was drafted; but in keeping with his faith, he was assigned to Camp Johnston in Jacksonville, Florida. He was made a Quartermaster, working in the camp headquarters. He was not sent overseas.

While serving in camp, he contracted influenza. He died on October 23, 1918. His body was sent back to his parents in Fresno and buried in the Liberty Veterans Cemetery.

It is not known if Royer ever worked in Stockton while with the land company. But his next of kin was his brother Clinton. Clinton lived in Stockton and worked in government service as a liaison to Holt Manufacturing.

ROY LINCOLN ESTES

Private – not assigned

On July 20, 1887, Roy was born to William M. and Adaline "Addie" Estes. William got a job as an attendant at the State Hospital in Stockton, so the family moved to that city sometime after Roy was born. The family resided at 328 E. Magnolia, just steps from the hospital. His mother was involved with the Temperance movement in Stockton. She stated in the 1910 census that she was an Institutional Leader.

On his draft registration, Roy stated that he was married to Jessie (Ollerich) and that he was a bookkeeper for M. Davidson, a produce company. Jessie was a nurse at St. Joseph's Hospital. Roy was well-known in Stockton as he had previously worked at Arthur Samuel's Smoke House, a popular cigar seller in town.

Roy enlisted in the Army in August 1918. He was sent to Fort McDowell for training. But two months into his training, he became ill with Spanish Influenza. He was moved to the Presidio in San Francisco for medical care. His parents and his wife were at his bedside when he succumbed to the disease on October 23, 1918. His body was sent to the crematorium at Park View Cemetery. At his family's request, no burial service was held.

VIVIAN ASHLEY DODD

Private – 88th Regiment, Australian Imperial Forces

Vivian Dodd was born December 17, 1897, in Australia to parents Hannah Usher and Richard Henry Dodd. In 1906, the family immigrated to California; and in the 1910 Census, they lived, in Palo Alto. By 1916, the Dodds are living at 236 W. Willow Street in Stockton. Richard was employed as the manager for the City Adjustment Company.

When Vivian completed his draft registration in 1917, he was working as a clerk for Holt Manufacturing. His older brother, compelled to serve prior to the United States entering the war, had enlisted with the British Expeditionary Forces and was fighting on the Western Front.

Vivian followed in his brother's footsteps and decided to join the Australian Imperial Forces. He enlisted and left San Francisco on October 12, 1918, at only 20 years of age. He was to report to the Imperial Recruits Depot in Windsor, Nova Scotia, prior to being sent overseas.

On the journey to Nova Scotia, Vivian became ill. When he arrived, he was immediately placed in the military hospital. He died of pneumonia on October 29, 1918. He was buried at Maplewood Cemetery in Windsor, Nova Scotia.

ELMER HAUB

Private – 159th Infantry

Elmer was born in Stockton on September 27, 1889, to George and Ida (Condy) Haub. In January 1898, Ida died of consumption. In the 1900 Census, Elmer and his siblings Aggie (Margaret), Ida, George and Eva were living in the West Oakland Foundling Home. Their father most likely was not able to care for the children and had placed them in the orphanage (which was common at the time).

Despite their early lack of parentage, the siblings made strides. By 1904, they were living back in Stockton at 219. S. Grant Street with their father. Based on city directories, it appears that the siblings lived together and supported each other by procuring jobs at an early age. At various times Elmer worked as a blacksmith at the Tool Works, as a gasoline engineer for Island Transportation Company and was employed at Holt Manufacturing.

Sometime in 1918, Elmer enlisted in the Army. He was sent to Camp Kearny as part of the 159th Infantry, which was created with National Guard units from California and Arizona and became part of the 40th Division. Elmer most likely did not ship out with his company when it left for Camp Mills at the end of July. He apparently was ill and sent back to Stockton. He died October 28, 1918, in French Camp at the County Hospital and was buried in the Rural Cemetery next to his mother in Block 20.

No public military demonstration could be presented the day of his funeral. At the time, Stockton was under quarantine because of the Spanish Influenza epidemic, so the mayor ordered Elmer's burial honors to take place graveside. A squad from the Home Guard presented a military salute and Taps was played by a member of the Record Carrier Boys' Band.

OLAF E. NELSON

Private – 91st Division

Olaf was born March 7, 1897, in Ishpeming, Michigan, to Lars and Ulricka. His parents had emigrated from Norway. At the time of the 1917 draft, Olaf was working as a shipping clerk for the Eastman Gibbon Company in Stockton. He resided at 920 E. Market Street, Apartment #7. His parents were still living in Michigan. Not much is known about Olaf. He was drafted and sent to Vancouver, Washington. He died on October 31, 1918, in the barracks, most likely of complications from influenza. His burial is unknown.

GLENN W. BUSH

Private – Company B, 82ⁿᵈ Infantry

Glenn was born in Hastings, Nebraska, on July 23, 1896, to John C. and Ella Clark Bush. He was one of eight children. John and Ella had married in 1893 while living in Colorado. They returned to Colorado Springs, residing there during the 1900 and 1910 US Census.

By June 1917, when Glenn completed his draft registration card, the family had moved to Stockton and was living at 1143 N. Center Street. Glenn was a clerk for Wilkes-Pearson-Knutson.

It is uncertain whether Private Bush served overseas. He died of Spanish Influenza on November 9, 1918, while stationed at Camp Kearny in San Diego. He was sent home to be laid to rest in Stockton Rural Cemetery. His parents later would be buried next to him in Block 37.

ROMAIN HERRICK SCHELL

Private – not assigned

Romain Schell was born in Knights Ferry, California, on January 28, 1890. His parents were Herrick and Clara Schell. In 1900, the family lived in Oakdale. On his 1912 voter registration, Schell stated that he was an electrician. When he completed his draft registration in June 1918 (our country's third draft), he worked as a linesman for the Sierra and San Francisco Power Company. He was married to Norma (nee McIntyre) and they lived in Manteca.

Romain was exempt from service since he was married. Wanting to serve, he waived his exemption. In late October, he boarded a train in Stockton headed for Camp Rosencrans in San Diego. Because of the influenza outbreak, the potential soldiers were asked to wear masks. Reportedly, Romain laughed it off and refused to wear the mask.

By the time the train reached San Diego, Romain was ill. He was sent immediately to the base hospital and died 10 days later, on November 4, 1918. That day, his wife and sister were on a train to visit him, but he died while they were traveling. Norma received a telegram telling her of his death when the two women reached the station in Los Angeles.

Romain's body was sent back to Manteca, and he was buried in Oakdale Citizens Cemetery.

OSCAR GULICK

Private – Headquarters, 1ˢᵗ Battery, 40ᵗʰ Coast Artillery Corps

Oscar was one of seven children born to Merari and Mary C Gulick. He was born April 20, 1894, in Stockton. The Gulick family lived in the Castoria Township near the small town of French Camp.

In the 1917 draft registration, Oscar was working as a farm laborer for the Tuxedo Land Company out of Stockton. He enlisted in the Coast Artillery Corps and reported to Camp Upton, New York.

The CAC was created to protect our country's coasts and provide local defense using heavy artillery, railway artillery and anti-aircraft artillery. Some of the American units were sent to France to operate alongside French forces to help protect France's coastal borders.

Private Gulick was attached to Headquarters, working in the barrack offices. Sometime in November 1918, he became ill, most likely from Spanish Influenza. He died November 18, 1918, in Brookhaven, New York. He originally was buried in the Yaphank Cemetery in Brooklyn. His body eventually was moved to Cypress Hills National Cemetery in Brooklyn, in Section 2 site 8619.

THOMAS SHIELDS DEHAVEN

Sergeant – Quartermasters, Aviation Corps

Thomas was born to Henry and Margaret Hughes DeHaven on April 25, 1893, in Briarton, Pennsylvania. In the 1900 Census, the family was living on a farm in East Fallowfield, Chester County, Pennsylvania. But in 1903, Henry died, so Margaret moved her young family to be with relatives in Sacramento, California. In the 1910 Census, they are living on "E" Street. By 1913, young Thomas was working as a bookkeeper for Pacific Telegraph and Telephone Company. The family had moved to 1609 16th Street in Sacramento.

While registering for the draft, Thomas was employed as a special agent for the Standard Oil Company in Tracy, California. He was living on East 8th Street in Tracy. He eventually would become manager of the Shell Oil Distributorship in Tracy. He was a member of the local Freemasons, Shrine and Eastern Star.

Thomas was drafted and chose to enter the Aviation Corps stationed at Kelly Field, San Antonio, Texas. Because of his skills, he was assigned to the accounting department (Quartermasters) and never was sent overseas.

In October 1918, Kelly Field experienced an outbreak of Spanish Influenza. Thomas came down with the dreaded disease, which eventually manifested as bronchial pneumonia. He never recovered and passed away on November 19, 1918. His body was sent back to Sacramento, where he was buried at East Lawn.

His rank is a bit of a mystery. His grave marker states he was a 2nd Lieutenant, but his death certificate signed by his commanding officer stated that he was a Sergeant. The latter most likely is correct.

WALTER LESTER SIEVERS

Private –61ˢᵗ Balloon Company, United States Aero Service

Walter was born on October 2, 1889, in Miranda, Faulk County, South Dakota to Charles Emil and Emma Mary (Rinder) Sievers. In the 1910 Census, the family was living in Hillsdale, Faulk County, working on its own farm. Sometime before he enlisted, Walter moved to Lodi, California with his brother Herbert and his sister Lillian, wife of C. E. Runnels.

Walter joined the US Aero Service and was attached to the 61ˢᵗ Balloon Company. He originally was sent to Fort Omaha, but later the company was transferred to Fort Crook, Nebraska. While training, Walter contracted influenza, which soon became pneumonia. He died on November 19, 1918. His body was sent home to the family plot in Miranda, South Dakota.

DOUGLASS LOUIS MESSERSMITH

Private – 91ˢᵗ Division (Spruce Production Division)

Douglass was born February 28, 1896, in Ottawa, Ontario, Canada to Charles Ollie and Alvina Henrietta Messersmith. They were immigrants from Germany. Douglass was the oldest son of six children.

In the 1910 Census, the family was living in Stockton at 1636 E. Market Street. Charles was working as a cupula tender at the Monarch Factory. At the time of the 1917 draft, Douglass was a baker for Van

Deusen Bakery on 437 Washington Street. By the end of 1917, Douglass had been hired by the Southern Pacific Railroad as a trucker for the Coast Division out of San Francisco.

Douglass was drafted and sent to Camp Lewis in Washington. The army naturalized him on August 8, 1918, making him a US citizen. While at Camp Lewis, he was assigned to the Spruce Production Division at Siemscarey, Washington. This division was responsible for harvesting spruce trees to be used in aircraft production. It was a major logging and manufacturing division of the Army, which had a contract with the Siems-Carey Company. The camp was built from September to November 1918 but was halted on November 11. Because of the timing, no actual lumber harvested was used in the war effort.

While working in the logging camp, Douglass came down with Spanish Influenza. He was moved to the hospital (temporary tent buildings) in Siemscarey for treatment.

Douglass sent a letter home telling his mother that he was very sick and that he hoped that the Army would send him home once he recovered. The letter did not arrive in Stockton until after his mother received the telegram notice of his death. He died of pneumonia on November 24, 1918, being only one of two soldiers who died at Siemscarey. His body was sent back to Stockton, and he was buried in Park View Cemetery in Manteca.

NOTE: Siemscarey is now part of Beaver, Washington.

VIRGIL ELLSWORTH PIERCE

Private – 4ᵗʰ United States Cavalry

Virgil was born in Eugene, Oregon, to Parley and Pearl Pierce on June 21, 1897. They moved to Zumwalt, Oregon, before the 1900 Census and later moved to Lodi, California. By January 1911, the Pierce family owned a restaurant and bowling alley in town. Of course, Virgil and his two sisters, Ardella and Stella, worked alongside their parents in the family business and were well-known about town.

Virgil decided to join the military prior to the United States entering the war. He enlisted in the United States Cavalry on February 10, 1917. He was transported to the Hawaiian Islands on April 13, 1917, as a recruit attached to the 4ᵗʰ Cavalry.

Private Pierce spent most of his military time in Hawaii; but towards the end of 1918, the unit was stationed in the Philippines.

In November, the 4ᵗʰ Cavalry was being transferred to Texas. While travelling through Arizona on November 5, the state went under quarantine due to the Spanish Influenza pandemic. While waiting in Douglas, Arizona, Virgil contracted the flu. It quickly developed into bronchial pneumonia. He died on November 27, 1918.

Private Pierce's body was sent by train to Lodi under military guard. He was buried with honors at Lodi Memorial Cemetery in Pioneer II, Plot 36A - Grave 18.

ORA FRANCIS WINN

Private – Base Hospital #29

Ora was born on December 20, 1895, in Downing, Schuyler County, Pennsylvania. His parents were George Washington and Rosetta (Minium) Winn. In the 1900 Census, the family was living in Independence, Missouri; and by the 1910 Census, they had moved farther west to Clifton, Colorado.

In the 1917 draft registration, Ora was farming with his father in Modesto. He stated that he was a Seventh-Day Adventist and was therefore a conscientious objector to the war. Ora was drafted and, in keeping true to his convictions, was assigned to a Base Hospital (#29) in Edmonton, Middlesex, England. He and other hospital staff arrived on July 6, 1918, on the *Empress of Russia*.

While serving in the hospital, he became ill, most likely from influenza. He died in December 1918 and was buried temporarily near the hospital. His body returned home on May 23, 1920, and he was interred in Lodi Memorial Cemetery next to his brother Otha, who had died in 1910.

AUGUST FREY

Private – Company 16 June Automatic Replacement

August was born in Trippe, McPherson County, South Dakota, on August 3, 1891. His parents were Phillip and Carolina (Lehr) Frey. He was one of 17 children born to the couple. In the 1900 Census, the family had moved a short distance to Kassel in McPherson County. By 1910, they resided in Elliott Township in San Joaquin County, in the small town of Victor.

In the 1917 draft registration, August lived in Victor and was a self-employed farmer. He was most likely drafted and sent to Camp Kearny as part of the June 1918 Automatic Replacement Draft. Private Frey departed for France on June 28, 1918, on the ship *Nestor* as part of Company 16.

August wrote home telling his mother that he had been having lung trouble. He was sent to the Walking Base Hospital #8 and then sent home on the ship *Kroonland* on November 26, 1918. But he did not make it back to the states. He died at sea on December 6, 1918, of tuberculosis.

Private Frey's body was returned to Lodi, and he was buried in Lodi Memorial Cemetery beside his mother, who died just days before he was transported. They are together in Pioneer 1, Block 67, Lot 1 and 2.

RICHARD NORTON COUPE

Private – 94th Aero Service Squadron

Richard was born near Challenge in Yuba County, California, to Henry and Catherine McTavish Coupe. Henry was a blacksmith working in Foster Bar. At age 18, Richard got a job as a hotel clerk in Slate Range, Yuba County; but by 1915, he was hired on as an apprentice brakeman for the Southern Pacific Railroad and assigned to the Fresno County crew.

In August 1916, Richard became a full-fledged brakeman and was sent to the Stockton Division. For awhile, he lived in the Southern Pacific Clubhouse and eventually found an apartment in Oakland. At the time of the 1917 draft registration, Richard was living in Tracy, California.

Upon enlistment, Richard was assigned to the 94th Aero Service Squadron. His unit left for France on October 27, 1918, on the White Star Line ship *Adriatic*. While serving in France, Richard contracted Spanish Influenza. He was shipped back to the United States in December, arriving in New Jersey on Christmas Eve. He was sent to the military hospital at Camp Merritt.

Richard never recovered from the influenza. It developed into pneumonia, and he passed away on January 21, 1919. His body was sent back to Yuba County. He was buried in the Sacred Heart Catholic Cemetery in Dobbins, California.

WILLIAM BRENNAN

Private – 19th Engineers, 91st Division
Private – 52nd Company, Transportation Corps

William was born on August 9, 1892, in New York City. His father was John J. Brennan, and his mother's name may have been Margaret. William had immigrated to New York from Ireland in 1881. In 1900, the family was living on Pacific Street in Brooklyn; but in the 1910 US Census, his father was a widower who resided on S. Center Street in Stockton. John was a grocer, and William worked at his father's store. William had three brothers, Joseph, Frank and Edward, and four sisters, Kate, Mary, Sarah and Anna. In 1915, William worked as a bellman for the Hotel Clark, and his brother Joseph was a clerk at the grocery store.

On his 1917 draft registration card, William wrote that he lived at 1147 S. Center Street and was a roundhouse foreman for the Santa Fe Railroad. He was most likely an early draftee. He was transported on April 17, 1918, on the ship *Chicago* bound for France. The ship's manifest stated he was a Private with the 19th Engineers out of Camp Lewis.

Private Brennan died sometime in 1918 of disease as noted in the "American Soldiers of World War 1." His body remained in France until June 20, 1919, when he was sent home from Bordeaux on the ship *Canandaigua*. On that manifest, he is attached to the 52nd Company Transportation Corps. It is not known where he was buried. Later, his siblings were buried in either the Stockton Rural or the San Joaquin Catholic cemeteries.

BERT LEWIS

Corporal – Company B, 30th Engineers

Bert was the son of Elizabeth J .Lewis. She married Henry Leiginger sometime between 1870 and 1880. Henry was a school teacher in Stockton. They had a son, William Henry, whom Bert listed as his next of kin.

Bert was a Corporal in Company B, 30th Engineers. He was transported to Europe on the ship *President Grant* on December 26, 1917. His early arrival indicated he either was an early enlistee or he already was serving in the military prior to the 1917 draft.

Military records state that Corporal Lewis died of disease sometime in 1918. He was buried in Belgium. On April 16, 1921, his body was sent to his brother, W. H. Lieginger, who lived in Stockton at 122 E. Jackson Street. It is uncertain where Corporal Lewis was buried.

An interesting note: There was another Bert Lewis from Stockton who served in Europe. He was Herbert W. Lewis, Jr., a local clothier. This Bert was a Sergeant First Class in the Repair Company, 825th Squadron of the AEF Aero Service.

FREDERICK D. POINDEXTER

Sergeant – Company K, 365th Infantry, 92nd Division

Frederick was born in Louisa County, Virginia, on July 10, 1888. He enlisted in the Army on April 3, 1912, and was sent overseas to Manila, Philippines. He served for three years as a Private in the 24th Infantry, First Platoon, 4th Squad Company M. This was a unit comprised of African-American soldiers. Private Poindexter arrived back in the states in San Francisco and was honorably discharged on April 17, 1915. He moved to Oakland, California, and got a job with the Southern Pacific Railroad as a porter. He later became a cook in a dining car for the Coastal Route out of Oakland.

In the 1917 draft registration, Frederick was working as a porter for the Manila Hotel, 9 S. El Dorado, in Stockton. He and his wife, Olivia, resided at 119 S. Center. He stated that his ethnicity was Ethiopian. He was 5'9" with dark hair, dark eyes and dark complexion.

Frederick was drafted (most likely due to his previous military experience) and sent to Camp Funston in Kansas. He was attached to the 92nd Division, an African-American division with representatives from all 48 states. The division adopted the buffalo as its insignia to honor the four Buffalo Soldier regiments of the US Cavalry in the 19th century. They became known as the Buffalo Soldier Division.

The 92nd shipped out of Hoboken, New Jersey, on June 10, 1918. Upon arrival in France, the Division was assigned to the French Army as support troops since the British and American forces did not want to serve in combat with men of color. They trained for trench warfare, but by August 1918, companies were being sent to the front line.

Frederick served in the 365th Infantry and was promoted to Sergeant in Company K. The 92nd was eventually assigned to the American Expeditionary Forces and saw combat during the last few days of the Meuse-Argonne Offensive. Its fighting mainly took place in November 1918 leading up to Armistice.

The 365th was sent back to the states on the ship *USS Olympic* on February 17, 1919. Although Frederick was listed on the ship's manifest, his name was crossed out, stating he had died of disease and was buried in France. His wife, Olivia, was next of kin, residing at 38 W. Sonora St.

On September 4, 1920, Frederick's body was returned to Olivia. It is not known where he was buried. She moved from Stockton in 1958, but returned to the area in 1968 when she married Luther Cayton. She died on March 3, 1971, in Contra Costa County.

WALTER LESLIE HUNTING

Private – unknown (perhaps the 28th Division)

Walter was born in San Diego County in July 1896 to Walter L. and Jane "Lou" Hunting. He was one of six children. In the 1910 Census, the family lived in Waterloo, just east of Stockton, where Walter Sr was working as a butcher. In the 1915 Stockton City Directory, Walter Jr resided at 1215 S. Center Street and worked as an auto trimmer.

Towards the end of the war, Walter decided to enlist in the Army. He was sent to Camp Hancock in Augusta, Georgia. This was the home of the 28th Division and was one of the largest military camps during the war. Due to its size, soldiers in Camp Hancock were exposed quickly to Spanish Influenza as it spread rapidly across the United States. Walter was not there long before he became ill. He died January 14, 1919. He was buried in the Stockton Rural Cemetery Block 37.

HARRY LEROY RICE

Private First-Class – Battery B, 147ᵗʰ Field Artillery

Harry was born in Oregon in August 1898. His mother was Marie "Mollie" (McLoughlin) and his father was Ralph Leroy Rice. In the 1900 Census, Mollie and Harry, who was 1 year old, lived with the Frank Chapman family in Yamhill, Oregon, where she worked as the housekeeper. Ralph and Marie divorced soon after the 1900 Census. When Harry was 11, Marie married William Warren. In 1910, the Warrens and the McLoughlins all lived together in Yamhill. Ralph was also in Yamhill and owned a butcher shop.

The Warren and McLoughlin families moved to Stockton, California. As a teenager, Harry found employment at the Sperry Flour Mill. In July 1917, Harry travelled to Portland and enlisted in the Army. He was only 18.

Harry was assigned to the 147ᵗʰ Field Artillery, which was originally part of the South Dakota National Guard. The 147ᵗʰ had been redesignated in October 1917 and needed recruits. Harry was attached to Battery B and found himself a soldier in the 41ˢᵗ Division.

Private First Class Rice and the rest of the 147ᵗʰ left New York on January 11, 1918, aboard ship transport #527. Harry listed his grandfather, Oliver P. McLoughlin, as his next of kin. Oliver lived at 1220 E. Market Street in Stockton.

While in France, the 41ˢᵗ Division fought in five campaigns including battles at Chateau Thierry, Verdun and the Argonne Forest. Harry survived the fighting and in November 1918 waited with his company to be transported back to the United States.

But Harry contracted influenza. His mother was notified in December that he had improved and would be coming home soon. But he took a turn for the worse and died of bronchial pneumonia in February 1919. He was only 20 years old. His mother, who now lived at 435 E. Mariposa in Stockton, was telegrammed of his death. It is unknown where he was laid to rest. Eventually, his family members all left Stockton and returned to Oregon.

MERREL ROY BATTILANA

Merchant Marine and Seaman Apprentice – United States Navy

Merrel was born May 17, 1900, to Guiseppe "Joseph" and Carlotta "Lottie" (Gianelli) Battilana in Stockton, California. In the 1910 Census, the Battilanas were living on S. San Joaquin Street and Joseph was a real estate agent in Stockton. In 1917, when Merrel completed his draft registration, his family had moved to a home at 1434 S. Hunter. Merrel was only 17 and stated that he was a student at Stockton High School.

Merrel decided to enlist in the Merchant Marines after his 18th birthday. Once the war ended, he enlisted in the Navy. He was stationed at Goat Island Naval Training Station in San Francisco when he contracted Spinal Meningitis. He came home to Stockton to recover, and after two months he returned to the Naval Station. Seaman Apprentice Battilana apparently had a relapse and died on May 22, 1919, just five days after turning 19 years of age. His father was by his side. He was buried in the San Joaquin Catholic Cemetery.

SIDNEY BROWN

Private – 316ᵗʰ Ammunition Train, 91ˢᵗ Division

Sidney was born in Stockton to Isaac and Fannie Brown in May 1890. "Ike" and Fannie were Polish Jews who emigrated from Russia in 1884. Ike was a tailor, and the family resided at 227 E. Lindsay Street. Sidney had three brothers, Leo, Raymond and Joe, and a sister, Ettie.

In the 1911 City Directory, Sidney was working as a clerk. His father owned a shoe store and tailor shop at 15 W. Sutter, so Sidney most likely worked in the family business.

Sidney was drafted and sent to Camp Lewis along with so many other young men from the area. He was attached to the 91st Division, 316th Ammunition Train and sent to France.

Sidney served at the Western Front until his unit was sent home in June 1919. On the transport home, he caught a cold. Upon returning to Stockton, his cold worsened. He died on June 11, 1919, being home only two days.

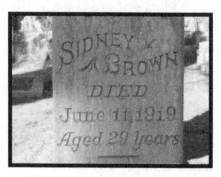

Private Brown was buried in the Congregation of Ahavas Achim Hebrew Cemetery in French Camp alongside his brother Raymond, who had died in 1913. Other family members also would be laid to rest there, including his father, who died May 13, 1926.

WILLIAM THOMAS LITTEBRANT

Brigadier General – United States Army, West Point Class of 1888

William Thomas Littebrant was born in Stockton on March 27, 1865, to Hartman and Catherine (Cunningham) Littebrant. Hartman was an early pioneer who arrived in Stockton in 1852. He owned several businesses along Main Street, including a livery business with George Aylesworth (operating a stage line to Placerville and Copperopolis) and a mercantile store with N. J. Salisbury. Hartman eventually would be appointed the director of the US Mint in San Francisco, a position he held until 1885, when he returned to Stockton and served as deputy sheriff for six years.

William attended grammar schools in Stockton and graduated from the Boys' High School in San Francisco. In 1884, he was accepted to West Point, where he graduated in 1888 and was commissioned a 2nd Lieutenant. He excelled in rifle and pistol shooting. He served on the Western Frontier in the 10th Cavalry assigned to Fort Apache. He rode alongside John Pershing, a fellow West Point graduate who would go on to be the Commanding General of the American Expeditionary Forces in Europe.

Lieutenant Littebrant married Laura Green of St. Louis in November 1890. She was the daughter of millionaire James Green, a clay products manufacturer. In 1891, Laura died from sepsis after giving birth to their twin daughters, Marian Emma and Laura Catherine. William wanted to stay in one place to help raise his children. So in 1892, he accepted a position as Professor of Military Science at the Missouri Military Academy. He resigned two years later to reenter active duty.

During the Spanish-American War, Littebrant was the Quartermaster of the 7th Cavalry. He became the commander of the regiment's Troop B while fighting in Cuba. When the war ended, he served in various troops in the 11th, 13th and 15th Cavalry, being posted in the Philippines until he returned to Cuba from 1908-1910.

In 1912, William graduated from the Army School of the Line, a graduate program for officers. He was promoted to Major and served as the Superintendent of Yosemite National Park with the 1st Cavalry. He also commanded the 1st Cavalry during the Pancho Villa Expedition along the US-Mexican border. In 1916, he was assigned to the 4th Cavalry and promoted to Lieutenant Colonel, overseeing recruitment in St. Louis, Missouri.

When the United States entered the World War, Littebrant was given the command of the 23rd Cavalry and promoted to Colonel. Early on, the regiment was reorganized as the 81st Field. Artillery. Colonel Littebrant requested training at Fort Sill, Oklahoma, to prepare for this transition from cavalry to artillery.

While at Fort Sill, Littebrant was promoted to Brigadier General, a temporary wartime rank, and given command of the 19th Field Artillery Brigade. The 19th was set to sail for France in December 1918, but the Armistice kept it stateside. Since the war had ended, William was reverted to his permanent rank of Colonel. He shared with friends that his failure to "get to the Front" was one of the greatest disappointments in his life. He was a career officer who yearned to give service.

Colonel Littlebrant was assigned the task of commanding Fort McClellan in Anniston, Alabama, overseeing the demobilization of troops as they headed home. His health had been taxed due to the strenuous training at Fort Sill. He died of lobar pneumonia on July 2, 1919. His attending Army Physician wrote: *"Death resulted from disease contracted in the line of duty."*

Colonel Littebrant was buried with full military honors at Arlington National Cemetery. He rests in Section 3 Site 4068. In 1930 Congress posthumously restored his rank to Brigadier General.

He was survived by his wife, Eveleen O'Keefe, whom he had married in 1910, and his daughters, Laura Catherine Clark Warren and Marian Emma Kealor Hunter. Eveleen was buried in Arlington beside William in 1947. Laura was buried in Arlington with her husband, Colonel George Stewart Warren, USAF. Marian was buried in Rye, Westchester, New York in 1944.

NB: Some information for the above was taken from Littebrant's biography written by Bill McKern, Arlington National Cemetery.

THOMAS B. THRELFALL

Private – Motor Transport Division

Thomas was born July 10, 1886, on the Threlfall Ranch just outside of Oakdale to William and Irene Threlfall. The family moved to Stockton, and in his 1917 draft registration, Thomas wrote that he lived at 348 S. California Street and worked as a teamster. He enlisted and left with a Stockton contingency on December 15, 1917. He had a working knowledge of automobiles, so he was sent to the East Coast for assignment. He arrived in France and was stationed at Gondrecourt, headquarters for the motor pool.

Private Threlfall had the responsibility of hauling ammunition to the front lines during both the St. Mihiel and Argonne offensives. It was during his time in the Argonne Forest that he contracted influenza. From Gondrecourt, he was sent to a base hospital.

Thomas battled the disease for many months. It developed into pneumonia, so he was transported back to the states on the ship *Leviathan* in April 1919. Upon landing in New York, Thomas was transferred to the United States Army Hospital in Aurora, Colorado, with the hope that the mountain air would mend his weakened lungs.

His mother was able to visit him, which lightened his spirits. She completed the paperwork to have him sent back to Stockton to undergo treatment with his local doctor. Sadly, he died November 14, 1919, from a pulmonary hemorrhage, never making it back to his home town. Instead, his body was sent by train, and he was buried in the Threlfall family plot in the Stockton Rural Cemetery alongside his father.

UNKNOWN CAUSE OF DEATH

EDWIN E. DARWIN

Sergeant – 26th Company, 166th Depot Brigade

Edwin was born in 1894 in Kansas. He married Hazel Weatherhead sometime between 1915 and 1916. Hazel was a young widow with a child named Vesta. According to Census records, their daughter Faye Luella was born in California on February 12, 1917.

Edwin was assigned to the Depot Brigade at Camp Lewis in the Public Works Division. It is uncertain when he arrived in Washington. He died at age 24 on December 15, 1918, of an unknown cause. He was buried in the Camp Lewis Post Cemetery, Section 1, Site E35. Hazel, as a young widow for the second time, would return to Kansas and live with her father and two young daughters.

Sergeant Darwin's connection to San Joaquin County is uncertain. But his name is etched on the plaque.

SYLVAN A .IRVINE

1st Lieutenant – Company F, 117th Engineers, 42nd Division

Not much is known about Lieutenant Irvine. His mother, Ethel, was listed as next of kin when he left on transport to France on October 18, 1917, aboard the ship *Covington*. The ship's manifest stated he was a private attached to the 117th Engineers, Company F. His mother's mailing address was P. O. Box 317, Stockton. The 117th Engineers was a California National Guard unit attached the 42nd Rainbow Division.

On November 23, 1918, his body was aboard the *USS Orizaba*, being listed as a 1st Lieutenant. The ship arrived in Hoboken, New Jersey, on December 2, 1918, and he was shipped to his mother, who now resided at 2406 College Avenue, Berkeley, California. His cause of death and where he is buried are unknown.

UNKNOWN MILITARY SERVICE

BYRON PURINTON

Unknown

George Byron Purinton was born in San Jose on April 21, 1888. His family moved to Stockton sometime before 1900, living in Waterloo just east of town. Byron lived in Barstow in 1910 and worked as a machinist for the railroad. During the 1917 draft, he lived in Buffalo, New York, and worked in the Engineering Department of Curtiss Airplane Company at the Elmwood Aviation Plant. His draft card stated he had been in Russia.

A passport was given to Purinton in 1914 to work in Russia for a two-year period. He stated he was an airplane mechanic. He returned to the United States in 1916. He had lived in Petrograd and worked with a Russian aero company.

It is unknown if he entered the military or when he died. But his brother named his son George Byron Purinton on September 25, 1917, most likely in his honor.

JOHN WILLIAM DALY

Unknown

John was born in Stockton on August 16, 1886, to Carroll Charles and Mary Daly. Carroll was a plumber. In 1900, the Daly family was living at 130 N. Union Street, where they remained until Carroll got a job offer in San Francisco. The family moved in 1909; and by 1910, John was working as a stenographer in a law office.

When John completed his draft registration, he was back in Stockton employed as a bookkeeper for the Harris Manufacturing Company. He resided at 510 E. Pinchot Street.

No information could be found regarding John's military service. He died on Christmas Day in Stanislaus County, 1918. He was buried in the San Joaquin Catholic Cemetery in Stockton.

PETER ROSCELLI

Unknown

There may be a mix-up regarding someone from Stockton reportedly killed in action. A death notice in The San Francisco Bulletin, July 1919, reported that Private Peter L de Roscelli of Stockton had been killed in October 1918 while on a recon mission near Gesnes, France. De Roscelli was a private in Company F, 361st Infantry, of the 91st Division.

But Private de Roscelli was transported back to the states on the ship *SS LaFrance* on December 24, 1918. The manifest states that he was wounded and was to be sent to Camp Merritt for further evaluation. Private de Roscelli was not from Stockton but from Hollywood, Los Angeles County. He would survive his wounds and spend time in the Los Angeles County Veteran's Hospital in 1933. He would later be given the Distinguished Service Cross for his valor and bravery. In 1942, he was working in Washington D.C. in the Government Printing Office.

If there was a Peter Roselli who died in the line of duty from Stockton, it may have been the young man who worked for the railroad. Peter Roselli was employed by the Southern Pacific Railroad, first in the Bridge and Building Division in 1916-1917 and then in the Maintenance Section in 1918. At one point, he was living in the Roundhouse in Tracy.

No further records, including military service, were found regarding him. The last railroad record was March 15, 1918.

MARTIN FREY

Unknown

The only records found on Martin Frey are a San Joaquin Voter Registration in 1912 and the 1920 Census. He resided on Daisy Street in Lodi and stated he was a farmer. This cannot be the young man who died in the line of duty in World War 1 since he is living in 1920.

LEWIS/LOUIS A .GRIFFITH

Unknown

There may be a mix-up with military records with regards to the death of Lewis A. Griffith, whose name is on the plaque honoring young men from San Joaquin County.

First – the only Louis A Griffith found in census records living in San Joaquin County was born January 12, 1895, in Lathrop to William George and Anita (DeWitt) Griffith. The parents divorced; and in 1910, William lived in Tracy and Anita was in Tulare township with her son Charles. Louis was not found in the 1910 census records. In 1917, he was living in San Francisco and worked as a waiter at the Clift Hotel on Geary and Taylor streets. No military service was located. Louis died June 15, 1919, in San Mateo. Burial information is unknown. But his siblings remained in the Lathrop/Tracy area.

Second- a Lewis A. Griffith was wounded while fighting in the Champagne area of France on November 1, 1918. He was a private in Company B, 310th Infantry in the 78 Division. But this young man had been born in Italy and enlisted in Rochester, New York. There is no connection to San Joaquin County.

Third – a Louis A. Griffith from Ohio was killed in action during the Meuse-Argonne Offensive. He may have been misidentified as being from San Joaquin County.

LLOYD TITUS

Unknown

Lloyd's name is on the World War I plaque for young men from San Joaquin County. No records have been found. There is a Lloyd Titus, from Michigan, who is buried in the Meuse-Argonne Cemetery. He served in the 126th Infantry of the 32nd Division. No connection to San Joaquin County has been discovered.

There is a draft registration from San Joaquin County for a William Leroy Titus from Lodi. But his registration was in September 1918, the "old man's draft." William was 43 and did not serve.

CARL ROBERT

Unknown

Carl Robert's name is on the plaque of men who died from San Joaquin County. No information has been found with such a name. A Carl Roberts was working as a machinist with the Southern Pacific Railroad in 1912, but no military service can be identified. There is a

Carl N Roberts from Ohio who died on November 4, 1918, in Ypres, Belgium. He is buried in Flanders Field American Cemetery. There was a Carl L. Roberts who joined the United States Cavalry in San Francisco and was transported to Hawaii on September 13, 1917, but no death nor connection to San Joaquin County can be established.

MISTAKEN DEATH

JOSEPH ARATA

Private – Company E, 361rd Infantry, 91st Division

Joseph Arata's name is not on the plaques, but he is found in the *American Soldiers of the Great War, Vol. 1* as a soldier killed in action, hailing from Stockton, California. But this may not be correct.

Joe was born in Santa Clara County on February 18, 1888. His family moved to Stockton sometime before 1912 when he was living with his father, John, at 329 N. California Street.

In the 1917 draft registration, Joe stated he worked on a farm in Modesto. He enlisted and was sent with an early contingency to Camp Lewis, where he was attached to Company E, 361st Infantry of the 91st Division.

His company was transported on July 6, 1918, aboard the ship *Scotian*. Their unit went to England for additional training prior to arriving in France in August. The 361st Infantry immediately was assigned to the reserve during the Battle of St. Mihiel from September 12-15. Soon after, the 361st found itself in the heart of the Meuse-Argonne offensive.

Joe's father, John, was sent a telegram notifying him of his son's death on September 29, 1918. The United States military has Joe killed in action. *The Stockton Record* reported his death and mentioned he was the brother of Caesar Arata, a local salesman.

But on January 19, 1919, Joe was transported back to the states on the *Manchuria*. The manifest stated he was among the sick and wounded and was to be sent to a hospital. It is quite possible Joe Arata from Stockton, California survived. There is a Joseph Arata, born in 1888, who was buried in the Casa Bonita Mausoleum in Stockton in 1972, next to a Caesar Arata.

WORLD WAR ONE AWARD RECIPIENTS

STOCKTON

Arthur Andrews	United States Citation
Frank Bates	United States Citation
Ben Cox	French Croix de Guerre
Phillip Tom de Martini	United States Citation
Alfred Fawke	United States Honorable Mention
Roland Gibbs	French Croix de Guerre
Sidney Gumpertz*	Congressional Medal of Honor
Ernest Hondaa	United States Citation
George Keddie+	French Croix de Guerre
Chester Mason	Belgian Croix de Guerre
Frank T. Mason	French Croix de Guerre and French Legion of Honor
Malcolm Minahen	United States Citation
William A. Palmer	French Croix de Guerre
Carleton Parker	United States Letter of Commendation
Karl E. Ross	Distinguished Service Cross
Peter Rosselli#	Distinguished Service Cross
Perry Schurr^	Distinguished Service Cross
Alva C. Thorpe	French Croix de Guerre
Andrew Vivasis	French Croix de Guerre

*Gumpertz lived in Stockton but moved to New York in his 20s
+Keddie's Cross was bestowed upon him by General Pershing
#Rosselli is probably a mistake – he lived in Hollywood, Los Angeles County
^Schurr moved to Orange County after the war

LODI

Bernard J. Jones	United States Citation
Carlton Lamberton	French Croix de Guerre
Clyde Needham	United States Citation

| Peter Sievers | Belgian Croix de Guerre |

CLEMENTS

| Oliver Wallace | Belgian Croix de Guerre |

ESCALON

| Cecil E. Thompson | Distinguished Service Cross |

RIPON

| Harold C. Strother | Distinguished Service Cross |

TRACY

| Paul Bushke | French Croix de Guerre |
| William Davis | French Croix de Guerre and United States Citation |

LINDSAY

| William J. Isley | United States Citation |

OTHER SAN JOAQUIN NOTABLE DOUGHBOYS

San Joaquin County had other young men who would survive the war and would continue to provide service to their country in a number of ways.

WARREN HENDRY ATHERTON

Captain – Ordinance Division

Atherton's life story is quite remarkable. He was born in San Francisco on December 28, 1891, to Dwight Copeland and Elizabeth (Hendry) Atherton. Dwight's father, the Reverend Isaac Atherton, was born in Maine and eventually served as minister to the First Congregational Church of Los Angeles from 1869 to 1871. Dwight was the foreman of an oil refinery and had married Elizabeth Hendry in 1886.

Elizabeth's father, William, was a blacksmith from Scotland who lived in San Francisco, where she was born in 1862.

Warren and his parents moved to Crockett in Contra Costa County sometime before the 1900 Census. This enabled Dwight to be closer to his workplace. Unfortunately, Dwight died on November 18, 1904, at age 40 of a heart attack. This left Elizabeth a young widow with a teenage son. She would never remarry, and so Warren would remain an only child.

Warren's father was a member of the San Francisco Masonic Lodge #361 and also a member of the Odd Fellows. These organizations may have been instrumental in helping young Warren find work.

At age 19, Warren was employed as a clerk for the Southern Pacific Railroad. He was living in Contra Costa County and renting a house. The 1910 Census stated that he had four young men boarding at the home and that Warren was the head of the household. He was the youngest man living at the residence.

Despite no formal higher education, in 1911, Warren was hired to clerk with a law firm in Stockton. He passed the California Bar in 1913. When Warren completed his 1917 draft registration card on June 5, he wrote that he was an attorney at law in the firm of HR McNoble and Atherton. He was single and lived at 1723 N. Commerce Street.

One month after completing his registration, Warren married Anne Holt on July 7, 1917. Anne was the daughter of inventor Benjamin Holt, who had developed the Caterpillar tractor. Holt and his brothers had founded the Holt Manufacturing Company.

On April 30, 1918, Atherton was transported to France aboard the ship *Kroonland*. He was a 1st Lieutenant in the Ordinance Division. Ordinance was part of the logistic team assigned to Headquarters that organized the disbursement of weapons and ammunition to the troops. It was no surprise that Lt. Atherton had landed in this position. The United States Government had a contract with Holt Manufacturing. In 1916, the British Army had placed an order for 1,000 Holt Model 75 gasoline-powered Caterpillar Crawler tractors. The United States added to that order and would use the continuous metal-belted Holt tractors to tow supply and ammunition trains across the boggy soil of France and Belgium. The 75 was particularly adept in hauling the six-inch howitzer and the Sixty Pounder to men fighting at the front. Newly promoted Captain Atherton would help oversee that task. His assignment also would put him in direct contact with General Pershing.

At the end of the war, Warren remained in France. He finally was transported back to the States on the ship *Calamares* on August 7, 1919.

Upon arrival, he was ordered to report to the Chief of Ordinance in Washington, D.C., where his wife's cousin Pliny Holt had been assisting the military with making design adjustments to the Holt tractors.

When Warren finally arrived back in Stockton, he returned to the practice of law. In the 1920 Census, he and Anne still were living at 1723 N. Commerce Street, and Warren had his own practice. By the 1930 Census, the Athertons, which now included four children, owned a home on Smith Tract, west of Stockton off Country Club Boulevard. This area would become known as Atherton Island.

In the 1937 City of Stockton Directory, Warren had created a law partnership with Barry McDermott. Their office was in the California Building at 11 S. San Joaquin. He eventually would become a judge and serve on the bench for a number of years.

He delved into civic affairs. He became president of the Chamber of Commerce. He was involved in the founding of the Jedidiah S Smith Society at University of the Pacific. He supported local organizations that were involved in education and the arts.

But his love was always the military. When he returned from World War I in 1919, the American Legion was being formulated. He was actively involved in the creation of the local Stockton legion. He eventually would become the national commander of the American Legion during World War II from 1943-44.

During his time as national commander, he would help write the Servicemen's Readjustment Act of 1944, otherwise known as the G.I. Bill. The bill provided services to those who had been on active duty for at least 90 days and had not been dishonorably discharged. This bill was in direct response to the difficulties faced by World War I veterans in their attempt to garner services, including monetary payouts.

Warren Atherton died in Stockton on March 7, 1976, leaving a legacy in his adopted hometown. He left his papers to University of the Pacific, and they are housed in the Holt-Atherton Special Collections department at the William Knox Holt Library. Warren Atherton Auditorium is home to the Stockton Symphony on the San Joaquin Delta College campus. The area around his home is still known as Atherton Cove. But his biggest legacy and probably the one he was most proud of, was to be considered the father of the G.I. Bill.

(Atherton's military photo is courtesy of Karl Ross American Legion Post 16. It hangs in the foyer of its building)

EDISON AMES HOLT

Sergeant – Headquarters, 304th Battalion, Tank Corps

Edison was the youngest child of Benjamin Leroy Holt and Anna Brown. He was born in Stockton on August 15, 1897, and had three older brothers and one sister (Anne Holt Atherton). His father was the inventor of the Caterpillar Tractor and was CEO of the Holt Manufacturing Company.

Edison attended Stockton High School from 1914-1918 and was actively involved in student government. Shortly after completing school, Edison joined the military. He was transported on the ship *Megantic* on October 20, 1918, less than 30 days from the war's end. It is apparent that Holt's attachment to the Tank Corps was in direct relationship to the contract Holt Manufacturing had with the United States Army. Additionally, he was sent to Headquarters to serve alongside his brother-in-law, Captain Warren Atherton. Edison most likely took orders from Colonel George S. Patton, who had been given command of the newly created Tank Corps.

When the war ended, Edison remained in France. On October 28, 1919, he applied for a passport to allow him to travel to London. In his application, he stated that he was a representative of the Farmers Loan and Trust and resided in Paris, attached to the American Expeditionary Force Headquarters. C. L. Neumiller, president of the Commercial Savings Bank of Stockton, was named as his reference. Included in the application was a letter from the manager of Caterpillar Tractor Ltd, 60 Queen Victoria Street, London, England, stating the company was looking forward to having Edison join the company as a representative of his father, Benjamin Holt. Edison apparently was being asked by his father to work at the subsidiary in London.

In 1920, Edison returned to Stockton and lived with his parents at 548 E. Park Street. At the time of the census, he was not employed.

Edison's father died in December 1920. The Holt Manufacturing Company had gone through several acquisitions and mergers. In 1925, it merged with its rival, C.L. Best, and became the Caterpillar Tractor Company. The main office was now in East Peoria, Illinois, and it was doing business in Canada, South America and Mexico. Additionally, offices were being created in San Antonio, Texas. Edison's brothers, William Knox and Alfred Brown, remained with the company along with their cousin, Pliney Holt. But Edison had other plans.

In 1927, Edison married Rose Marie Brunn. Her father, Harold Brunn, was a successful surgeon in San Francisco. Edison and Rose Marie moved to San Francisco. In the 1930 Census, the couple has a son, Edison Jr., and resides at 68 Presidio. Edison was now an investment broker. By 1932, his brother Albert had joined him in Holt and Company Stockbrokers on 111 Sutter Street. Edison and Rose Marie now had a daughter named Elsie and still lived on Presidio.

Being raised in an entrepreneurial family had rubbed off on Edison and his brothers. In 1933, Holt and Company added real estate to its portfolio. It now had offices at 1180 Market Street in San Francisco and in Marin County and Redwood City. Other members of the family came to work for the brothers. And in 1937, Edison diversified again, adding Stringer Storage Company to his list of businesses. He was president of the storage company and took on a new partner with his stock brokerage, now called Holt & Ede, with William Ede, Jr. named as president. The brokerage was now at 235 Montgomery Street.

In 1937, Rose Marie's mother had died, so the Holts went to live with Dr. Brunn, whose home was at 2821 Jackson Street. They were still living at the residence during the 1940 Census.

Edison died on February 8, 1964, at his home in Marin County. But he never forgot his Stockton roots. He was buried in Stockton Rural Cemetery along with so many of the Holt family.

HAROLD CORBETT STROTHER

Corporal – Company L, 362nd Infantry, 91st Division

Harold was born in Salida on April 11, 1896, to William and Dolly (Ellenwood) Strother. The family had a farm in the rural area between Salida and Ripon in San Joaquin County.

In the 1917 draft, Harold stated he worked on the family farm. He may have enlisted, as it appears he was an only son. Harold trained at Camp Lewis and was assigned to the 362nd Infantry of the 91st Division. He was transported to France on the *Empress of Britain* on July 6, 1918. At the time, he was attached to Company E, according to the ship's manifest. Eventually, he was transferred to Company L and promoted to Corporal.

On October 31, 1918 near Steenbrugge, Belgium the following took place: "*Advancing under heavy machine gun fire with the aid of two other soldiers, Corporal Strother silenced the fire of a strongly fortified machine gun position which caused severe losses in the ranks. His action made possible the further advance, not only of his own platoon, but also the company on his left.*"

Based on the above stated recommendation from his commanding officer, Corporal Strother was awarded the Distinguished Service Cross for extraordinary heroism in action.

With the war's end, Harold waited to return to the States. He finally was transported on the ship *Floridian* on April 3, 1919, and assigned to Camp Mills. He was demobilized from Mills and returned to rural life in Ripon.

In 1922, he was hired as an agent for the Union Oil Company in Chico, California. He had married, so he and his wife, Cecelia, set up their home in Butte County. His parents decided to leave Ripon and follow him to Chico. In 1924, he was transferred to Siskiyou County, where he lived the remainder of his life. He died on August 28, 1968, and was buried in Mt. Shasta Memorial Park.

PERRY NELSON SCHURR

2ND Lieutenant – Company C, First Gas Company, Chemical Warfare Service

Perry was born in Greencastle, Indiana, on March 12, 1882. When he was 18, he traveled to Denver, Colorado, and enlisted in the Army. He was attached to Company E of the 9th Infantry and fought in the Philippines during the Spanish-American War. He saw heavy action and was one of only 14 men in his company to survive. After serving three years, he was discharged in February 1903.

Perry re-enlisted in Plattsburg, New York, on November 13, 1903, and joined the 5th Infantry, Company H. He was promoted to the rank of Sergeant and assigned to Fort Niagara. His unit was sent to China and fought in the Boxer Rebellion. Perry was discharged for a second time on July 12, 1904, at Madison Barracks, New York Harbor. Notes on his discharge papers state his character was excellent.

Perry found work in Santa Ana, California, with the Southern

California Edison Company. He married Lydia Foster, and they moved to Salt Lake City, where their son Donald was born in 1908. Perry continued to be employed as a lineman. In the 1910 Census, they lived on 10th Avenue in Seattle with their 2-year-old son. Perry was now a lineman for the Seattle Street Car Company. By 1917, he had been hired as an electrician for the Western Gas and Electric Company in Stockton and resided at 1016 El Dorado Street. He and Lydia now had two sons and a daughter.

Perry was too old for the June 5, 1917, draft. But with his soldier's background, he felt compelled to enlist, which he did in Stockton on November 13, 1917. Lydia took the children to Orange County, California, to be with her parents.

Sergeant First Class Schurr was assigned to Company C of the 30th Engineers in the 2nd Battalion. He was in the 1st Gas Company in the American Expeditionary Forces Chemical Warfare Service. Three other local young men: George Keddie of Stockton, D. L. McPherson of Stockton and W. H. Killiam of Modesto, were also in this company. Known for their tin hats and gas masks, these young men were responsible for rescuing the injured while bullets and shrapnel spewed about them. Six weeks after landing in France, they found themselves in almost constant motion, seeing action in 39 of 42 days.

During his time in battle, Sergeant First Class Schurr was wounded four times. In September 1918, during the interaction at St. Mihiel, he was hit in the leg by a shell splinter. On September 30 during the Meuse-Argonne offensive, he was shot in the wrist, with the bullet going clean through. Then on October 4, he was hit in the head by a gas shell. On October 18, he was gassed while rescuing comrades on the front line. He was recognized for gallantry with a commission as lieutenant. He *"worked in the midst of a severe barrage saving the lives of many wounded by prompt first aid and transporting the worst cases to the nearest dressing station."* For this, he received the Distinguished Service Cross. Additionally, he was awarded a Purple Heart and two Oak Leaf Clusters.

Once the war ended, Lt. Schurr was transported back to the States on the ship *Wilhelmina* on February 11, 1919. The manifest states that he was ill with pleurisy. He arrived back in Stockton with McPherson and joined the Veterans of Foreign War Luneta Post 52. They both returned to their jobs at Western Gas and Electric.

Since Lydia had remained in Orange County with the children, Perry quit his job in Stockton and moved to Santa Ana. He was hired as a lineman for the Electric Light Company as stated in the 1920 Census. Unfortunately, Lydia died in 1923. Since Perry's job took him on the road, the children went to live with their maternal grandmother.

Perry apparently continued to have physical difficulties stemming from his injuries. He spent time in the Veteran's Hospital in Los Angeles. By the 1940 Census, he was living in the Veteran's Home. He died in Los Angeles on October 25, 1957, and was buried in the V. A. Cemetery of Los Angeles. He rests in Section 294, Row A, Site 20.

SIDNEY GUSTAVE GUMPERTZ

Sergeant First Class– Company E, 132nd Infantry, 33rd Division

Sidney was born on October 24, 1879, in San Rafael, Marin County, California, although some records state he was born in Stockton. By the 1880 Census, his parents, Gustave and Julia, lived on California Street. Gustave was a partner with M.S. Arndt in the Arcade Clothing Company.

Sidney spent his formative years in Stockton. But in 1900, Gustave decided to move the family to Syracuse, New York. Sidney was 20 at the time and was a cashier at a clothing store. In 1901, he and his father owned the Union Shoe & Clothing Company in Buffalo, where he managed the store. While in Buffalo, he joined the New York National Guard. In September 1901, Sidney was appointed as a military escort to President McKinley's body after he was assassinated in Buffalo.

By 1905 at age 25, Sidney had moved into Manhattan and found work as a real estate agent. Most likely having wanderlust, he moved again – this time to Chicago. In the 1910 Census, Sidney stated he worked in advertising. While in Chicago, Sidney married his wife, Anna. Records show that the couple moved back and forth between Chicago and Manhattan.

When the United States entered the war, Sidney enlisted from Chicago. With his previous military experience, he was appointed First Sergeant to Company E of the 132nd Infantry, attached to the 33rd Division.

While in Europe Sidney wrote Letters from the Yanks, which were published by *The Stockton Record*. Readers were proud to say they knew the soldier when he was a young man growing up in town. His writings were honest and sometimes graphic, but they provided the citizens with a glimpse of what our doughboys were experiencing.

Sergeant Gumpertz fought with bravery and valor. On September 29, 1918, near Bois-de-Forges in the Argonne Sector, he was cited by his commanding officer for his actions. *"Charging through a dense smoke screen and a murderous barrage of artillery and machine gun fire and capturing single handed a machine gun crew of 19 Germans was a remarkable achievement in itself. But when a few days after the same doughboy duplicated this feat with a second bag of prisoners running up to eleven he surely is entitled to some recognition."* The soldier on either side of him was killed, but he continued on undaunted until he was face to face with the enemy. In two days, he captured 30 German soldiers and disarmed two machine gun nests. Gumpertz was awarded our nation's highest military accolade, The Congressional Medal of Honor.

Sidney lived a long life. He died on February 16, 1971, and was buried in the Long Island National Cemetery. He rests in the Distinguished Service Section, Site 65.

FUNERAL SERVICES

When one of Stockton's sons came home to rest, the city honored him. Mayor Oullahan would order flags flown at half-mast, and the local dignitaries would fall into action. Unfortunately, they would get too much practice in organizing a funeral service.

First, a call would go out to local fraternal organizations and social clubs. Military units would be requested to attend. Churches would be contacted, and The Record would print the notice and other details.

The Holt Caterpillar band would be asked to play. Many of their former members already had lost their lives in battle or from disease. The local Veterans of Foreign War, Stockton's Home Guard, the Grand Army Veterans, and Veterans of the Spanish-American War would participate. Members from various fraternal organizations would send representatives (or actively participate if the young man had been a member), such as the Odd Fellows and the Rebekahs, the Masonic Lodge, Native Sons of the Golden West, Woodmen of the World, Anteros Club, and the Battery C Mothers. When some of the young men were exhumed in France and returned to Stockton in 1921-22, the newly created American Legion Post 16 (Karl Ross) would take over the task of performing the military rituals.

The Women's Relief Corps would assist in organizing the funeral cortege. They would provide flowers, often fashioned in the shape of the American flag with a gold star resting in the blue field. Mare Island would send pall bearers if the young man had served in the Navy, while the Stockton Army Recruitment Center would provide participants if the fallen was a soldier in the Army.

Local churches would provide the songs, and often an entire church choir would sing. Merchants along the line of the march were asked to close their doors respectfully as the group passed. At the end of the service, the procession would follow the casket to the place of burial: Stockton Rural Cemetery, San Joaquin Catholic Cemetery, Park View Cemetery in Manteca and the Congregation of Ahavas Achim Jewish Cemetery in French Camp, the latter two requiring participants to board the train.

As a writer for *The Stockton Record* wrote on September 30, 1918, "God rest the souls of these boys, our young patriots and heroes, who have made the supreme sacrifice for their country." The citizens of Stockton agreed.

BURIALS

AMERICAN CEMETERIES IN FOREIGN COUNTRIES

Aisne-Marne, Belleau France

| Private Vaughn J. Kiefer | Plot B | Row 1 | Grave 7 |

Brookwood, Surrey England

| Private Fred Livermore | Tablets of the Missing |

Flanders Field, Waregem Belgium

Corporal Thomas W. Hugill	Plot C	Row 2	Grave 22
Sergeant Karl E. Ross	Plot B	Row 1	Grave 3
Private Jack Ayk	Plot B	Row 4	Grave 18

Meuse-Argonne, Romagne France

Private James B. Anderson	Plot A	Row 31	Grave 14
Private John G. Anderson	Plot F	Row 28	Grave 32
Corporal Harold E. Cary	Plot B	Row 32	Grave 12
Private Frank W. Elsholz	Plot B	Row 34	Grave 18

Sergeant Carl R. B. Gustafson	Plot D	Row 13	Grave 31
Corporal Edward H. Lorensen	Plot D	Row 14	Grave 7
Corporal James H. Mead	Plot G	Row 27	Grave 35
Corporal Clyde W. Needham	Plot E	Row 30	Grave 17
Philip Sherlock	Plot C	Row 35	Grave 1
Corporal Harold A. Sexton	Plot A	Row 43	Grave 21
Private FC Oliver J. Stedman	Tablets of the Missing		
Private Henry A. Thorson	Plot D	Row 17	Grave 9
Sergeant Will I. Tredway	Plot B	Row 25	Grave 15
Corporal Earl Woodward	Plot H	Row 34	Grave 9

Oise-Aisne, Saringes-et-Nesles France

Private Gasparo P. Cabutto	Plot A	Row 33	Grave 4
Private Alexander Linde	Tablets of the Missing		
Private Darrell C. Mitchell	Plot C	Row 7	Grave 22

Somme, Bony France

Private James R. Miller	Plot C	Row 14	Grave 2

St. Mihiel, Thiaucourt France

Private Frank R. Patnoe	Plot A	Row 22	Grave 28
Corporal Alan/Allen W. Stone	Plot D	Row 22	Grave 10

Ligny-St Flochel British Cemetery

Private Walter Bicknell	Section 111	Grave E19

Maplewood Cemetery, Windsor Nova Scotia, Canada

Private Vivian A. Dodd

NATIONAL CEMETERIES

Arlington National Cemetery, Arlington Virginia

2nd Lieutenant Loui C. Beauman	Section 2	Site 2398
Brigadier General William T. Littebrant	Section 3	Site 4068
Private Olien O. Rhodes	Section 18	Site 1052

Cypress Hills, Brooklyn New York

Private Oscar Gulick	Section 2	Site 8619
Fireman 3rd Class Louis LaFarque	Unknown	
Fireman 2nd Class Harry L. Mercer	Section 2	Site 792

Rosencrans, San Diego California

Bugler Charles R. Curry	not known

San Francisco, San Bruno California

3rd Mate James E. King	Plot N	
Sergeant George L. McCall	Plot A	Site 1246
Clyde Stamper	Plot A	Site 117

Santa Fe National Cemetery, Santa Fe New Mexico

| Private Philip (Felipe) B. Montoya | Plot A-1 | Grave 1187 |

MILITARY CEMETERIES

Camp Lewis Post Cemetery

| Sergeant Edwin E. Darwin | Section 1 | Site E35 |

Fort Sheridan Post Cemetery

| Private Oscar S. Mortensen | Section 5 | Site 434 |

HOMETOWN CEMETERIES

Lodi Memorial, Lodi California

Private August Frey	Pioneer I	Block 67	Lot 1
Sergeant Ralph W. Gillespie	Pioneer I		
Private Herbert Hovard			
Cook George Mauch			
Lieutenant Charles R. Patten			
Private Virgil E. Pierce			
Private Roy V. Setzer			
Private Arthur J. Spencer	Pioneer II	Block 26	Lot 1
Private William V. White	Mausoleum		
Private Ora Winn			
Private Charles W. Wisthoff			
Private Henry Wittmeier			
Private Arthur Vincelet			

Park View Cemetery, Manteca California

Herbert Boyer	Private Cornelius Harrison
Private Karl I. Bradigan	Sergeant Clinton McCausland
Quartermaster Paul E. Carrier	Private Douglass Messersmith
David C. Cottrell	Private Cecil E. Thompson
Private Roy L. Estes	Corporal Lester L. Weylandt
Private First-Class Percy J. Fischer	

San Joaquin Catholic, Stockton California

Seaman Apprentice Merrel Battilana	Fireman 3rd Class Earl Hickey
Private Joseph G. Campodonico	Private Edmund T. Kasper
Private First-Class John Casenave	Private Adam Klein
Private Charles Fontanella	

San Joaquin Congregation of Ahavas Achim Hebrew Cemetery

French Camp California

Private Sidney Brown

Stockton Adas Yesharan Hebrew Cemetery, Stockton California

Private Joseph Drabkin

Stockton Rural Cemetery, Stockton California

Electrician 3rd Class Millard F Brown		
Private Glen Bush	Block 37	
Private Vern Dragoo	Block 26	
Private William A. Fisher	Block 17	Grave 26
Private Elmer Haub	Block 20	
Private Walter L. Hunting	Block 37	
Private George Pahl	Block 224	Grave 57D
Private Dewey D. Sivley		
Private Thomas Threlfall		

Linden Cemetery, Linden California

Corporal Guy W. Staples

Tracy Public Cemetery, Tracy California

Private James G. McDermott

Oakdale Citizen's Cemetery, Oakdale California

Corporal Herbert H. Adams

Modesto IOOF Cemetery, Modesto California

Private Frank E. Sperry

Elk Grove-Cosumnes Cemetery, Elk Grove California

Corporal Charles Eric Walther

East Lawn Cemetery, Sacramento California

Sergeant Thomas DeHaven

Mountain View Cemetery, Oakland California

Hospital Apprentice Harold Higgins   Plot 48

Mountain View Cemetery, San Bernardino California

Corporal Paul Holdzkum

Holy Cross Catholic Cemetery, Colma California

Private Martin Troy, Jr. (memorial)   Section 95   Plot L   Grave 13

Visalia Public Cemetery, Visalia California

Walter J. Halstead   Section A   Block 25   Lot 2

Sacred Heart Cemetery, Dobbins Yolo County, California

Private Richard N. Coupe

Morris Hill Cemetery, Boise Idaho

Bugler Bernard Irwin   Section J3   Row 6   Grave 3

Lincoln Memorial Cemetery, Portland Oregon

Private First-Class, William Schleiger

Miranda Cemetery, Miranda South Dakota

Private Walter L. Sievers

Alva Cemetery, Alva Wyoming

Private Henry Gage   Lot 6

Habberton Cemetery, Habberton Arkansas

Private William E. Stone

Greenwood Cemetery, Shreveport Louisiana

Private Ernest Bates

Marionville IOOF Cemetery, Marionville Missouri

Sergeant Hope L. McFall

UNKNOWN

Lieutenant Charles Chilton Moore

1st Lieutenant Sylvan Irvine

Sergeant Frederick Poindexter

Private William Brennan

Private Walter W. Figgins

Sergeant FC Bert Lewis

Private Olaf E. Nelson

CONCLUSION

In 1917, when the United States entered the Great War, the young men of our country were faced with a momentous task. The war brought a sense of duty. Patriotism ran high. Our soldiers believed in the words of President Wilson: "***The world must be safe for democracy. Its peace must be planted upon the tested foundations of political liberty.***" The doughboys accepted the challenges in front of them. Yet in meeting those challenges, so many would make the supreme sacrifice.

In Flanders fields the poppies blow
Between the crosses, row on row
That mark our place; and in the sky
The larks, still bravely singing, fly
Scarce heard among the guns below

We are the Dead, Short days ago
We lived, felt dawn, saw sunset glow,
Loved and were loved, and now
We lie in Flanders fields.....

Major John McCrae,
Brigade Physician, CEF
(1872-1918)

ADDENDUM

Company L of the 363rd Infantry had many young men from San Joaquin County. Most were transported on the *Benalla* while others were later assigned to this company.

Stockton – Savio Joseph Fugazzi*, Laslo Ghiglieri, John Dixon Sterling, Henry Ledtke, Andrew Delucchi, Hans Merz, Albert Peterson, Harold Sexton*, Herbert Adams*

Lodi – Albert Daniels, Sisto Albiani, Thomas Hugill*

Escalon – Carl Gustafson*, Edward H. Lorensen*

Manteca – James Rawleigh, Ben Buckhout, Hope McFall*

Ripon – Clinton McCausland*

Tracy – Elmer Branch

Clements – Oliver Wallace

*denoted killed in action

IMPORTANT TERMS:

American Expeditionary Forces (AEF): The term follows how other countries described their national army. The Canadians were the Canadian Expeditionary Forces (CEF); the Brits were the British Expeditionary Forces (BEF). It signifies an army that is sent abroad to fight.

Automatic Draft Replacement: The Army began holding drafts in the cantonment training camps to fill holes in other divisions. The holes had been created from men discharged or injured who could not fight overseas. The 91st Division at Camp Lewis had men whose names were drawn as replacements. Many went to the 4th Division at Camp Greene, South Carolina, and to the 41st Division at Camp Funston, Kansas.

Doughboys: This is an informal term used during World War I that denotes members of the AEF who served in the Army or Marines. There are many theories explaining the nickname, but no one is certain how the term came to be. The name was used prior to World War I, but during that time-frame *doughboy* was popularized.

BIBLIOGRAPHY: MOST RESEARCH DONE ONLINE

Abmc.gov (American Battlefield and Monument Commission)

Ancestry.com

US Census, City Directories; World War I Draft Registration Cards; California World War I Soldier Citations; US Dept of Veteran's Affairs BIRL; World War I Casualty Listings; American Soldiers of World War I; California World War I Death Announcements; World War I Service Cards and Photos; Railroad Employment Records; US Army Transport Service Passenger Lists 1910-1939; Birth, Baptism and Christening Records; California Death Index

Find-A-Grave.com

Honorstates.org

Legion.org (American Legion)

NIH.gov (National Institutes of Health) information regarding Spanish Influenza

Personal Papers of Aubrey E. Dixon

The Stockton Record – April 1917 to December 1923 (microfiche San Joaquin County Library)

Tinkham, George H., *History of San Joaquin County, California*; Los Angeles, Calif. 1923

Wikipedia.com

Worldwar1centennial.org

91st divisionleague.org

ABOUT THE AUTHOR

Elaine Dixon-Ugarkovich was born and raised in San Joaquin County. She grew up in Thornton, graduated from Galt High School and attended University of the Pacific. She earned her B.A. in 1975 and her M.A. in 1983. She earned her Administrative Services Credential from California State University, Stanislaus in 2004.

Elaine spent 31 years in education, teaching in San Joaquin County for most of that time. She taught students with learning disabilities, gifted students, students in alternative programs and general education. Her final years were spent working as a Program Specialist for Manteca Unified School District. She retired in 2005.

Her passions are travel, historical fiction and nonfiction, music, and genealogy. She is an avid Oakland A's fan and enjoys watching a great game of hockey. She loves to cook (and eat) homemade pasta and previously won several baking awards at the San Joaquin County Fair. Her rose garden is a tribute to her grandmother, whom she thanks for her green thumb.

She has been married to her husband, William, a retired Stockton firefighter, for more than 37 years, and they have a grown son.

Made in the USA
Las Vegas, NV
17 November 2020